Local Government In Western Nigeria: Abeokuta, 1830-1952

August 1 2013

Local Government In Western Nigeria: Abeokuta, 1830-1952

A Case Study Of Exemplary Institutional Change

For Fredy Gonzalez
A young man of promise

thank you for valuing
All my creative efforts.

Dr. Akinniyi Savage

To order additional copies of this book, contact:
Xlibris Corporation
1-888-795-4274
www.Xlibris.com
Orders@Xlibris.com
67985

CONTENTS

FOREWORD...ix
PREFACE..xi
ACKNOWLEDGMENTS xv

CHAPTER

I. HISTORICAL FOUNDATION AND CONCEPTUAL
    FRAMEWORK...1

II. THE YORUBA IN WESTERN NIGERIA AND THE
    ADVENT OF THE BRITISH...17

        The Yoruba in Western Nigeria 18
        The Egba before 1865 21
        The British in Nigeria and the Arrival of the Saro.............27
        The Impact of the British on the Egba 31

III. THE EGBA SARO AND THE ALAKE AS INSTRUMENTS
     OF INSTITUTIONAL CHANGE IN ABEOKUTA 51

        The Egba United Board of Management, 1865-1874 51
        The Egba United Government, 1898-1914 55
        Alake Ademola II 58

IV. THE STRUCTURE AND PRACTICE OF NATIVE
    ADMINISTRATION IN ABEOKUTA.................................85

        The Egba Central Council (1939-52) Up to 1946 86
        The Period of "Progressive" Unions................................92
        The Alake Goes into Voluntary Exile 93

The Alake Returns to Abeokuta 100
The Local Government Law of 1952 103

V.   SUMMARY AND CONCLUSIONS 115

GLOSSARY...129

BIOGRAPHICAL ENTRIES...141

CHRONOLOGICAL HIGHLIGHTS OF EGBA HISTORY 143

SUMMARY LIST OF EGBA FIRSTS IN NIGERIA...................147

BIOGRAPHICAL SKETCHES OF EGBA ELITE......................151

REFERENCES..225

APPENDICES 243

INDEX..247

To my parents:

Modupe and Akinbomi,
who are my progenitors to the new elite;
as well as to my brother, Akintunde,
with whom I share the legacy.

The local government law for the Western Region of Nigeria was passed in 1952. This signaled the gradual movement of some members of the new elite away from Abeokutan politics and on to regional politics in Ibadan. However, the new elite's importance to Abeokuta was crucial. They created an indelible mark on the political institutions of Abeokuta.

In conclusion, the process of democratization changed not only the political institutions in Abeokuta but also the type of personnel of those institutions. These changes in the institutions of Abeokuta were brought about by members of the new educated elite. Before the arrival of the new elite in Abeokuta, government was a closed society for the traditional elite. By 1952, government was open to every constituency in Abeokuta. This presaged the comprehensive democratization movement in Nigeria. The process of democratization in Nigeria should resonate with all those in the African Diaspora, because members of the new elite would have been able to approximate their achievements in Abeokuta, had they immigrated into Europe and the Americas voluntarily.

Akinniyi Savage, Ph.D.
May 12, 2009

ACKNOWLEDGMENTS

The completion of any book necessarily accumulates a myriad of psychological debts. My first debt, both severally and collectively, is to the triumvirate of Drs. Ross E. Dunn, Charles Smith, and Charles H. Cutter, all of San Diego State University, California, USA, who were nascent influences in the writing process of this book.

It is with pleasure that I express my gratitude to my cousin Prince Olusunmade Akin-Olugbade who redacted portions of my manuscript and insisted on the imperative of my maintaining only a superlative quality for such a work. He was a fountain of knowledge during this project. My brother, Michael Akintunde Savage, Esq., also assisted me immeasurably by being my contact person for all points of information in Nigeria. I could not have completed this book without his invaluable and expeditious coordination.

Accolades are also extended to my former colleagues Dr. Ruth Sowby, Ronald W. Johnson, Jane Y. Ding, and Peter Han, previously of DeVry University, West Hills, California, for their interest and encouragement during the embryonic years of the writing process. The approbation of one's peers is valuable academic capital to harvest and infuse into the frisson of composing a manuscript. Moreover, Susan McDonald, Associate Dean of Academic Affairs at DeVry University, Sherman Oaks, California, deserves credit for first extolling the virtues of my writing my own history book.

Bouquets are offered to thank all the staff members of the Inglewood Public Library in California. Particularly, my gratitude is directed toward Franklyn J. Francis of the main library who patiently ferreted out various books for me through interlibrary loans; to Mrs. Ulla Davis, senior librarian; and to

Ms. Rosalind Cannon and Ms. Brenda James-Craig of the Morningside Park branch who assiduously ensured that I gained access to their best facilities.

Very apropos in its timeliness was the contribution of cousin Pamela Savage whom I wish to thank for providing the information that I requested concerning her late husband, and my godfather, Hon. Justice William Akibo Savage. Ms. Debbie Perry of Power Ford, Torrance, California, USA, is also to be thanked for verifying the debut of Ford Thunderbirds to ensure that my memory was not askance.

Also with warm affection, I offer my belated hearty appreciation to the family of Dr. S. Olajire Olanlokun, the erstwhile chief librarian, and to the library staff of the University of Lagos, Nigeria. It was very serendipitous to renew my acquaintance with Dr. Olanlokun who, when I met him in his cavernous office asking for assistance with the biographical section of my book, very enthusiastically reminisced about our graduand years at the University of Lagos. Dr. Olanlokun died very unexpectedly on March 31, 2006, and was buried on April 21, 2006. May his soul rest in perfect peace!

Penultimately, I want to trumpet the many contributions of my fictive kin: Brother Julius Akin Edoh, of Puyallup, Washington, USA; Hon. Pearl Quinones, the erstwhile board president of the Sweetwater School District, California, USA; Dr. Olukemi A. Wallace, my "healing hands" physician who has a medical practice in Hawthorne, California, USA; and Mrs. Modupe Somotun, of Lawndale, California, USA, for their continual encouragement in the certitude of the completion of this book. Akin Aboaba, of New York, New York, USA, was particularly generous in providing primary material on his great-great-grandfather, Chief Aboaba. Plaudits are also due to Diane Gaylor, who through meticulous diligence unearthed numerous references for my utilization, and to Jeffrey Gorup, both of DeVry University, Los Angeles, USA.

In coda, kudos are due to Danielle Ridley, of California State University, Northridge, California, USA; prophet (Dr.) Emmanuel Alonge, pastor of the New Light Christ Apostolic Church, Los Angeles, California, USA; Adebisi Bamgbade of Lagos, Nigeria, who took the photographs of modern Abeokuta proximate to the publication of this book; and to Journey Bonnie Basic and Travis Meyer, former students of mine at DeVry University, West Hills, California, USA. They are hereby acknowledged with gratitude for their editorial assistance in the completion of this book.

CHAPTER 1

HISTORICAL FOUNDATION AND CONCEPTUAL FRAMEWORK

Abeokuta has had a variegated administrative history on its way to becoming the capital of Ogun State in western Nigeria. No other town in western Nigeria has gone through the gamut of local government forms in quite the same way. From its creation in 1830, Abeokuta has passed through rule by chiefs and elders, kings, democratic councils, and finally from the 1950s onward, a constitutional monarchy with various combinations of local power groups forming the *de facto* governing body. The succession of local government forms has not always been a linear progression toward more efficient government leading to greater modernization. Abeokuta, by the 1940s, however, had sufficiently advanced administratively to be considered one of the most efficient local government bodies in western Nigeria.[1]

The purpose of this book is to delineate, specifically, the democratization process of government institutions in Abeokuta during the 1940s and 1950s. It is the manner in which this was achieved in Abeokuta that made it so important. We are primarily concerned with the rise and fall of the king of Abeokuta and how this process was affected by the various political factors in Abeokuta. More than any other town in western Nigeria, Abeokuta evidenced an enlightened leadership and a percipient administrative policy in the 1940s. Progress and development in western Nigeria seemed to lie with the abrogation of the system of a single ruler and the democratization of the basis of the administration in the provinces. This was also the case in Abeokuta because, despite its leadership, new sociopolitical groups arose to challenge the status quo. The political savvy exhibited by Abeokuta elicited the superlative statement that Abeokuta was "the model for all the other native administrations in the Western Province of Nigeria."[2] The seminal importance of Abeokuta was articulated in 2005, during the coronation of the tenth and regnant Alake of Abeokuta, Oba Michael Adedotun Gbadebo III. On this occasion, President Obasanjo noted that Baptist Boys High School, Abeokuta, specifically, had produced two national presidents (if we include Bashorun M. K. O. Abiola), governors, and Obas.[3] We are not concerned here so much with a comparative study as to how Abeokuta acquired its "model" status as we are with its further modernization after 1939. Since the central theme concerns itself with the internal politics of Abeokuta, only slight references are made to other towns in western Nigeria.

The period under study is that which saw the introduction of native administration to western Nigeria. The point of emphasis of the study started in 1939 with the creation of the Western Provinces of Nigeria and the introduction of native administration to Yorubaland.[4] This was a particular and local application of the theory of indirect rule. This system was the mode of government inaugurated in Nigeria by Lord Lugard, whereby government was to be perceived by the people as emanating from the local dignitaries while really originating with British political officers. Native administration was necessitated as a system of government by the exigencies of staffing and finance in which Lugard found himself upon appointment as governor-general of Nigeria in 1914.[5] The period under study ends in 1952 with the inception of the local government act for western Nigeria, which was an attempt by the new regional government to usher in a new era of local administration.

Before discussing Egba politics in the twentieth century, it will first be necessary to identify the broad political factors at work in Abeokuta and in Nigeria. It will also be pertinent to identify Abeokuta as a geographical expression and to describe its traditional mode of government. It will further be necessary to provide a description of Abeokuta's administrative development from its inception in 1830 to the creation of provinces in Nigeria in 1939 by the British.

The specific factors that shaped Abeokuta's political development are five in number. The first factor is that Abeokuta enjoyed the unique privilege of formal independence from Britain between 1898 and 1914. Secondly, the pivotal sociopolitical group, the intelligentsia, had a continuity of purpose and achievement in Abeokuta.[6] Thirdly, the king of Abeokuta, Alake Ademola II, was the most progressive ruler in western Nigeria during the 1940s and 1950s. Fourthly, the women of Abeokuta, as an organized sociopolitical aggregate, played an active and effective role in the government at this time. Lastly, Abeokuta followed, more closely than any other Nigerian town, the example of Lagos, the then capital of Nigeria.[7]

Some general factors were also at work in the 1940s and 1950s. Nationally, two factors stand out. The first is that Nigeria was moving toward self-government, leading to independence. Secondly, this process was directed by the intelligentsia of the country.[8] Locally, two elements are important. In an administrative sense, Abeokuta was moving from a government based on a "sole native authority" to government through a "chief in council."[9] This was in common with several other towns.[10] Furthermore, the intelligentsia was enjoying an increased governmental role.

Western Nigeria between 1939 and 1952 (which then included the present Lagos, Ogun, Oyo, Osun, Ekiti, Ondo, Edo, and Delta states) stretched from between the Niger delta in the south, through the tropical rain forest, rolling plains, and savannah in the center, to the desert in the north. It covered an area of 45,376 square miles, or slightly more than one-eighth of the total area of Nigeria, which is 356,669 square miles. By 1950, the population of this area consisted of 6,114,000 Nigerians and 2,900 expatriates. The dominant ethnic group was the Yoruba, the then third largest ethnic group in Nigeria, after the Hausa and Igbo groups. Presently, Yoruba is spoken by approximately 20 percent of Nigerians (second only to Hausa, which is spoken by about 21 percent of Nigerians).[11] The Yoruba—with their tradition of urban life and complex economic, political, and social structures—for more than a century were dominant among the Nigerian elite, as they provided school teachers, doctors, clerks, and other white-collar workers both for Nigeria and for its neighboring countries.

The term "Yoruba" is generally ascribed to the group of people who occupy the present western part of Nigeria. The Yoruba view themselves as having

very distinct intragroup ethnology while generally acknowledging a common
ancestry. Abeokuta, with which we are concerned, was founded by the Egba
group among the Yoruba. In this exposé, the term "ethnic group" is used to
describe the superordinate Yoruba as a racial and cultural entity while the
appellation "ethnicity" is reserved for the Egba, the specific populace within
the Yoruba. The ancient town of Abeokuta was situated amidst a group of
Precambrian rock formations, the most prominent of which is the famous
Olumo Rock. Abeokuta was the third largest populated town in western
Nigeria during the period under study. It had an area of 1,869 square
miles and a population of 272,000 people.[12] It was described archly by one
Englishman as "a mass of corrugated iron roofs, glaring beneath the huge
outcrop of gigantic rock where the founders first settled."[13] Modern Abeokuta
is located forty-eight miles northwest of Lagos. It is about three hundred
feet above sea level, exuding a hot, humid climate with an average annual
rainfall of forty-seven inches. The geographical coordinates for Abeokuta
are 7° 9' 39'' N by 3° 20' 54'' E. Today, Abeokuta is a growing metropolis
with a population of 406,500 that is the capital of Ogun State.[14] The polis
is divided into four sections: Egba Alake comprising of forty-five townships,
Egba Oke-Ona with seven townships, Gbagura (Egba Agura) consisting
of seventeen townships, and Egba Owu encompassing three townships.
Contemporary Abeokuta is an agricultural trade center for rice, yams, cassava,
corn, palm oil and palm kernels, cotton, fruits, and vegetables. It is also an
exporting point for cocoa, palm produce, fruits, and kola nuts.[15]

The following discussion will present the two broad racial groups most
in evidence in western Nigeria during the period under study: the Yoruba
and the British. The history of the Yoruba will be traced briefly. The
Egba will be identified within the Yoruba, and their history described.
The political development of Abeokuta rested on the interaction of three
sociopolitical hierarchies: the king of Abeokuta, the traditional elite, and
the new intelligentsia. The elite of the Ogboni, Ologun and Parakoyi, and
the new elite of the repatriated emancipated slaves, known as the Saro, will
be discussed. Two groups among the British will be identified. These are
the political officers and the missionaries. The impact of the British on the
Egba at Abeokuta will also be examined.

SUGGESTIONS FOR FURTHER READING

Achebe, Chinua. *Things Fall Apart*. Oxford: Heinemann Educational Publishers, 1958.

————. *Arrow of God*, New York: Anchor Books, 1969.

Ajayi, J. F. Ade. "The Continuity of African Institutions under Colonialism." *Emerging Themes of African History*, pp. 190-199. T Ranger, ed. Nairobi: East African Publishing House, 1968.

Afigbo, A. E., et al. *The Making of Modern Africa*. 2 vols. Academic Press; London: Frank Cass, 1986.

Ali, Taisier M., and Robert O. Matthews, eds. *Civil Wars in Africa: Roots and Resolution*. Montreal: McGill-Queens's University Press, 1999.

Amadi, L. O. *Dictionary of Nigerian History: From Aba to Zazzau*. Bethesda, MD: International Scholars Publications, 1998.

Bever, Edward. *Africa*. Phoenix, AZ: Oryz Press, 1996.

Burton, Sir Richard Francis. A*beokuta and the Cameroon Mountains: An Exploration*. London: Tinsley Brothers, 1863.

Coleman, James S. *Nigeria: Background to Nationalism*. Berkeley: University of California Press, 1971.

Curtin, Philip S. *Africa Remembered: Narratives by West Africans in the Era of the Slave Trade*. Madison, Milwaukee: The University of Wisconsin Press, 1967.

Cutter, Charles H. *Africa 2002*. 37th ed., pp. 78-83. Baltimore: United Book Press, 2002.

Fage, J. D. *A History of Africa*. New York: Routledge. 3rd ed., 1995.

Falola, Toyin. *The History of Nigeria*. Westport, Connecticut: Greenwood Press, 1999.

———. *Culture and Customs of Nigeria*. Westport, Connecticut: Greenwood Press, 2001.

Gibbs, James. *Wole Soyinka*. Westport, Connecticut: Greenwood Press, 1988.

Gilpin, Robert. *Global Political Economy: Understanding the International Economic Order*. Princeton, NJ: Princeton University Press, 2001.

Ihonvhere, Julius. *Africa and the New World Order*. New York: Peter Lang Publishing, 2000.

Ikime, Obaro, ed. *Groundwork of Nigerian History*. Ibadan: Heinemann Educational Books for Historical Society of Nigeria, 1980.

Iliffe, John. *Africans: The History of a Continent*. New York: Cambridge University Press, 1995.

Jones, Eldred Durosimi. *The Writings of Wole Soyinka*. London: Heinemann, 1983.

Maier, Karl. *This House Has Fallen: A Journey through Nigeria's Heart of Darkness*. New York: Public Affairs, 2000.

Maja-Pearce, Adewale, ed. *Wole Soyinka: An Appraisal*. Oxford: Heinemann, 1994.

McIntosh, Susan K., ed. *Beyond Chiefdoms: Pathways to Political Complexity in Africa*. New York: Cambridge University Press, 1999.

Metz, Helen Chapin, ed. *Nigeria: A Country Study*. Washington, D.C.: U.S. GPO. 5th ed., 1992.

Mwakikagile, Godfrey. *The Modern African State: Quest for Transformation*. Huntington, NY: Nova Science Publishers, 2001.

Nebo, G. N. *Nigerian Commercial Policies*. Enugu State, Nigeria: Immaculate Publications, 1999.

Nwafor, James C. *Nigeria in Maps*. London: Hodder and Stoughton, 1982.

Olanlokun, Olajire. *The Legend: Sir Ahmadu Bello*. Lagos, Nigeria: Literamed Publications (Nigeria), 2001.

———. *The Legend: Obafemi Awolowo*. Lagos, Nigeria: Literamed Publications (Nigeria), 2003.

Overland, James H. *Sources of Twentieth-Century Global History*. Boston: Houghton Mifflin Company, 2002.

Oyewole, Anthony. *Historical Dictionary of Nigeria*. Lanham, MD: Scarecrow Press, 1998.
Reader, John. *Africa: A Biography of the Continent*. New York: Alfred Knopf, 1998.

Shillington, Kevin. *History of Africa*. New York: St. Martin's Press, 1995.

Soyinka, Wole. *The Swamp Dwellers, 1959.*

———. *The Lion and the Jewel, 1959.*

———. *The Trials of Brother Jero, 1960.*

———. *The Interpreters, 1965.*

———. *The Road, 1965.*

———. *A Dance of the Forest, 1966.*

———. *Kongi's Harvest, 1967.*

———. *Madmen and Specialists, 1970.*

————. *Season of Anomy, 1973.*

————. *Collected Plays* (including *A Dance of the Forest, The Swamp Dwellers, The Strong Breed, The Road, The Bacchae of Euripides*), 1973.

————. *Collected Plays 2, 1975.*

————. *Myth, Literature and the African World, 1976.*

Stewart, John. *African States and Rulers.* Jefferson, NC: McFarland & Company, 1999.

Sutherland, Dorothy B. *Enchantment of the World: Nigeria.* Chicago: Children's Press, 1995.

Tumano, Tekena N. *The Evolution of the Nigerian State: The Southern Phase, 1898-1914.* London: Longman, 1972.

Wright, Stephen. *Nigeria: Struggle for Stability and Status.* Boulder: Westview Press, 1998.

INTERNET RESOURCES

The following Internet sites contain written and visual materials that are germane to this chapter.

African Studies: Nigeria
<http://www.columbia.edu/cu/lweb/indiv/africa/cuvl/NRhist.html>
Retrieved February 26, 2003

Biography of Samuel Ajayi Crowther (1807-1891), an Egba and the first African Anglican bishop
<http://www.gospelcom.net/chi/BRICABRF/crowther.shtml>
Retrieved August 18, 2002

Global Literacy Project—Global Citizens—Classroom. "Nigeria—History since 1960"
<http://www.glpinc.org/Classroom%20Activities/Nigeria%20Articles/Nigeria-History%20si . . . >
Retrieved February 26, 2003

His Majesty Oba Alayeluwa Oyebade Lipede, the Alake of Egbaland
<http://abeokuta.freeservers.com/cgi-bin/i/akande/Lipede.jpg>
Retrieved August 17, 2002

History of Nigeria
<http://www.countryreports.org/history/nigehist.htm>
Retrieved February 26, 2003

Incisive interview with Professor Wole Soyinka, an Egba and the first African Nobel Prize winner in literature
<http://globetrotter.berkeley.edu/Elberg/Soyinka/soyinka-con1.html>
Retrieved August 18, 2002

Nation by Nation: History of Nigeria
<http://www.nationbynation.com/Nigeria/History1.html>
Retrieved February 26, 2003

Overlooking Abeokuta
<http://www.uni.edu/gai/abeokuta_pictures/view_4.jpg>
Retrieved August 17, 2002

Panoramic view of Olumo Rock, the predominant geographical feature of
    Abeokuta
<http://www.uni.edu/gai/abeokuta_pictures/Abeokuta.jpg>
Retrieved August 17, 2002

Photograph of Olumo Rock
<http://www.uni.edu/gai/abeokuta_pictures/hill_Abeokuta.JPG>
Retrieved August 17, 2002

Photograph of Olusegun Obasanjo, Nigerian president (May 29, 1999,
    to the present)
<http://us-africa.tripod.com/nigeriaobasanjo.jpg>
Retrieved August 17, 2002

Photograph of the Ogun River as it runs through Abeokuta
<http://www.edu/gai/abeokuta_pictures/View_rock.jpg>
Retrieved August 17, 2002

Political Map of Nigeria, 2002
<http://us-africa.tripod.com/nigeriamap.gif>
Retrieved August 17, 2002

Sample of a man's shirt made of traditional material (*adire* or tie-dye)
    from Abeokuta
<http://www.molli.org.uk/explorers/colls_objects/robe_pop.htm>
Retrieved August 19, 2002

Scaling Olumo Rock
<http://www.uni/gai/abeokuta_pictures/crack_Abeokuta.jpg>
Retrieved August 17, 2002

St. Peter's Cathedral, the oldest church in Nigeria
<http://abeokuta.freeservers.com/cgi-bin/i/akande/stpeterscathedral.jpg>
Retrieved August 17, 2002

(formerly the University of Lagos, Abeokuta campus), which specialize in science, agriculture, and technology, and the Ogun State Polytechnic (built in 1979). The 1996 population estimate of Abeokuta was 427,400 people.

Rice and cotton were introduced by the missionaries in the 1850s, and cotton weaving and dying (with locally grown indigo) are now traditional crafts of the town.

Abeokuta is the headquarters for the Federal Ogun-Oshin River Basin Authority with programs to harness land and water resources for Lagos, Ogun, and Oyo states for rural development. Irrigation, food-processing, and electrification projects are included. Local industry is limited but now includes fruit-canning plants, a plastics factory, a brewery, sawmills, and an aluminum-products factory. South of the town are the Aro granite quarries, which provide building materials for much of southern Nigeria, and a huge, modern cement plant at Ewekoro (18 miles south).

Ascension to the summit of the massive outcrop of granite rock that forms the landmark Olumo Rock is now made easier by a modern elevator constructed by the Ogun State government. Scaling the Rock is also enhanced by an artistic iron staircase. Renovations to the site's infrastructure were completed in 2006. These modernization projects included a new museum, restaurants, and a water fountain.

The 2005 estimated population of Abeokuta was 593,140 people.

CHAPTER 2

THE YORUBA IN WESTERN NIGERIA AND THE ADVENT OF THE BRITISH

In this chapter, we will identify the Yoruba in western Nigeria and the advent of the British to Nigeria. The political development of Abeokuta was directed by these two racial groups. The generic term "Yoruba" envelopes several ethnicities who view themselves as being distinct ethnocentric and political groups. They are, however, bonded with one another through their homophyly, which attests to their mutual antiquity. The origins and early history of the Yoruba will be sketchily drawn. The Egba are an ethnicity within the Yoruba. Abeokuta is their home city. In an African context, a town is often viewed as a separate country; hence, when we talk about Abeokuta, we will refer to it as a city-state. We will trace the history of the Egba from their several towns in the homeland to their move to the metropolis of Abeokuta in 1830.[1] We will continue their history up to 1854 and the emergence of a strong king. In the 1830s and 1840s, groups of émigrés started arriving in Abeokuta. These were repatriated, manumitted slaves from Sierra Leone and Brazil. Those from Sierra Leone came to be known as the Saro, and those from Brazil as the Amaro. We will trace their inception in Abeokuta. The last group that we will be concerned with is the British. From a foothold in West Africa at Sierra Leone in 1787, the British moved along the coast of West Africa, arriving in Nigeria in 1849. We will describe how they became established in Nigeria up to 1914 and show their influence in Nigeria and, particularly, on Abeokuta.

The Yoruba in Western Nigeria

There are a number of theories as to how the Yoruba arrived at their present-day location.[2] The most repeated tradition of migration is that the autochthonous Yoruba arrived in Nigeria in four distinct groups, starting perhaps as early as 2,000-1,000 BC (according to one of the first assessments) with the last group starting to migrate from northeast Africa, probably around the beginning of the eighth century.[3] They subsisted on agriculture in urban settings.

Community is very important among the Yoruba, as is veneration for age and its perceived, attendant, gerontocratic virtue—wisdom. There is a family hierarchy that is designed to ensure homeostasis in a household. Children are expected to respect their parents; spouses should respect each other. The female spouse is paramount in household matters while the male partner is generally responsible for overarching family affairs. Kinship is paramount.[4] Oyeronke Oyewumi, a feminist, proffers the nuclear family as being the basis for a definition of family structure in Nigeria. In concurrence with Niara Sudarkasa, a social anthropologist, Oyewunmi asserts that "it is the lineage that is regarded as the family. The lineage is a consanguineously based family system built around a core of brothers and sisters—blood relations." Hence, neolocal residency is very prevalent. Escalating conflicts among family members are normally addressed by those best suited to resolving them within the family with last resort lying with the extended family head. This structure is carried through to the society as a whole. The Oba is the head of an ethnicity and is expected to maintain comity in his sphere of influence.

There is also a hierarchy in spiritual matters.[5] Olorun is the god of the Yoruba, and he is responsible for the creation of the universe as the Olodumare through the use of his ase—divine power.[6] Reverend Omosade Awolalu affirms that "it is rare, if not impossible, to come across a Yoruba who will doubt the existence of a Supreme Being, or claim to be an atheist. If there is anyone like that, further investigation will reveal that he has been exposed to non-African cultural influences."[7] The religion of the Ifa Oracle constitutes the ontological understanding of Olorun.[8] Ifa divination of Olorun's will is based on an interpretation of odu—a sacred unwritten assemblage of religious, as well as social, and philosophical knowledge—by a babalawo, a sacerdotal Ifa functionary. Below Olorun are several orisas, who, as deities for every conceivable idea or physical entity, perform a variety of universal and pragmatic tasks. Professor Biobaku posits that there are no fewer than 401 gods in the pantheon of Yoruba traditional religion.[9] Even today, sacrifices are expected in propitiation of the gods, although the form of propitiation has transmogrified from killing domesticated animals, such as goats and cows, to graft. The gods and goddesses who pervade the cosmology, depending on one's locality, include Olumo (Abeokuta), the god of protection; Ogun, the god of iron; Sango, (Oyo), the god of thunder; Osun, the god of rivers; Aje, the god of wealth; Yemoja, the goddess of the sea; Oya (Offa [Sango's wife]) the goddess of rivers; Oro (Iseyin), the god of bravery; Agemo (Ijebu), the god of prosperity; and Esu (Satan), the god of energy.[10] Abimbola emphasizes that "Esu is a neutral force in the universe that controls both the benevolent and the malevolent supernatural powers. He is the universal policeman."[11] The theocracy extends from worshippers to priests, ancestors, spirits, gods, and finally to Olorun, for divine intervention.

The Yoruba see their "countries" as extended families, and their political organization is patterned as such. Hence, the Yoruba constitute a collectivist society. The general title for king in Yorubaland is "Oba." The Oba was the father of the country, and the subjects were the children. The Oba, a crowned head, exercised jurisdiction over the affairs of the country. Government was a sort of constitutional monarchy on a democratic base. Apart from the Oba, Yoruba political administration incorporated and combined representation on the basis of residential quarters with the representation of social interest groups.[12] To represent the views of the people to the Oba, there were the town's hereditary and nonhereditary chiefs, family heads, quarter heads, guild heads, heads of age-groups, as well as representatives of the town's women and immigrant elements.

The specific title of the king of Abeokuta is "Alake." The Alake was the overlord of the whole city-state.[13] He was also the head of the Ake section within the city-state. Succession to the Alakeship was restricted to the royal family of the Ake section and not thrown open to the whole town, as was the case in some other Yoruba towns.[14] Each of the four sections in the city-state managed its own affairs and, therefore, had its own sectional Oba. Today, however, as a result of miscegenation, most sections of Abeokuta do in fact share in the rotation for ascendency to the Alakeship.

An Oba had a variable number of men in constant attendance. They not only saw to his personal comfort but also were his messengers and representatives for

official as well as private purposes. The Oba of a Yoruba town, in theory, was
an omnipotent ruler. In practice, however, he was advised by his chiefs and had
to take their opinions into consideration when making decisions. The *de facto*
instruments of authority in a town were really the chiefs, councils, lineages, and
associations. The most powerful traditional association in Abeokuta was the
Ogboni Society. While the "Ogboni" was the name given to the judicial body
of some Yoruba towns, the Ogboni in Abeokuta was, in addition, the chief
society that held real power in each section of the town. Secret proceedings
and blood oaths ensured the solidarity of the Ogboni Society.[15]

The Ogboni system was a highly developed institution by the Egba. Made up
of important personages—both men and women—its function was to serve
as a nexus between the Oba and his people. Ideally, the system restrained
Obas from being despotic while ensuring that the governed eschewed
anomie.[16] In fact, the Ogboni constituted court and council, selected and
controlled chiefs, and preserved custom and tradition. It was the executive,
legislative, and judicial body of each Abeokuta township and, when strong,
of the city-state of Abeokuta itself in a single entity.[17]

Almost all men in Abeokuta are believed to have entered the Ogboni
association or cult. Some rose to titled office through the payment of fees and
with the consent of the members of higher grades.[18] Vacancies in the iwarefa,
the highest grade of six chiefs (later known as the Alake's inner chiefs), were
filled through election by the remaining chiefs who were members of the
grade immediately below it. The membership of the iwarefa was distributed
equitably among the descent groups in Abeokuta. Two intermediate groups
later developed identities of their own. These were the Olorogun (Ologun)
chiefs, who were in charge of the formation of the army, and the Parakoyi,
who supervised trade and formed the local chamber of commerce.

Having identified and discussed briefly who the Yoruba are and what their
political structure is, it will now be pertinent to provide a background
history of the Yoruba, and particularly of the Egba, the ethnicity within the
Yoruba with which we are most concerned. The establishment of Ile-Ife is
recognized as the earliest expression of Yoruba culture. Oral tradition has it
that this town was founded by the mythical figure known as Oduduwa (the
progenitor of the Yoruba). The Yoruba established their rule from Ile-Ife
over the original inhabitants (about whom little is known), creating new
settlements as they moved southward.

One of these settlements was Old Oyo, started between 1388 and 1431 by Oranmiyan, the son (or grandson) of Oduduwa, who is thought to have founded a new dynasty in Benin, farther south.[19] Old Oyo became the center of a Yoruba empire, the Old Oyo Empire, where effective political power was discharged, while Ile-Ife became the spiritual center of the Yoruba people. The head of the empire was known as the alafin. Stretching from the land of the Ga (in present-day Ghana) in the west to Idah in the east, and from close to Zaria in the north to practically the Atlantic coastline in the south, the empire lasted for four centuries. The basis of the empire was the strength of its army. The Are-Ona-Kakanfo, the supreme commander, became an exalted chief within the empire.

By the middle of the sixteenth century, the Old Oyo Empire had grown beyond its optimum size, given the difficulties of communication and control between the metropolis and the provinces. Civil war broke out (1754-1774) when Gaha, the Bashorun, or prime minister, usurped the throne of the Alafin. It was during this period that a leader arose among one of the tributary people in the empire, the Egba. According to Professor Biobaku, the foremost authority on the Egba, this leader, Lisabi, took the opportunity to gain independence for the Egba from the Oyo yoke.[20] Other provinces of the Old Oyo Empire also secured their independence at this time. Lisabi became the "Lycurgus of the Egba," as he taught them how to remain free and how to govern themselves.[21]

The Egba before 1865

The word "Egba" (contracted from "Egbalugbo") means "the wanderers toward the forest." The original Egba territory, known as the homestead of the Egba, was a series of about three hundred towns from the River Oba in the north to Ebute-Metta (presently a neighborhood of Lagos) in the south, and from the Osun River in the east to Ipokia and the River Yewa in the west.[22] This was the area circumscribed by the people of Oyo to the north, the Ijebu to the south and southeast, the Egbado (wanderers to the river) to the southwest, the Ketu to the west, and the people of Ile-Ife and Ijesha to the east. Egba territory in the middle of the eighteenth century included the important towns of Ibadan and Ijaye, occupied by refugees from the Oyo Empire.

The Egba towns were ruled as a federation, divided up into three provinces. In the north were the Egba Agura (or Gbagura) with their Oba, the Agura.

The Egba Oke-Ona were situated to the south, near the Ijebu. Their Oba was the Osile. The third province was that of the Egba Alake in the southwest. This was originally called Egba Agbeyin (the last to arrive), which was at first subject to an outside authority, the Ojoko of Kesi.[23] The people of this area later chose one of their own, the Alake, ruling from Ake, as their monarch. Among the provincial Obas of the Egba, the Alake gained ascendancy, followed in importance by the Osile and the Agura. These three Obas were crowned kings, although each town in the provinces had its own tributary Oba. Many of the original Egba towns have long since vanished, although Iddo and Ebute-Metta (both Lagos localities) still flourish. This organization of the Egba suggests three distinct migrations, each one moving farther south toward the Atlantic Ocean. Egba traditions look to Ile-Ife for the origin of their towns. Indeed, Ajalake, the first prominent chief, is said to have been a son (or grandson) of Oduduwa; hence a possible reason for his ascendancy as the senior Oba among the Egba.

Cultural and governmental evidence point to the fact that the Egba were indeed under the aegis of the Oyo Empire. When this first took place is not clear. Professor Biobaku asserts that it was a question of Oyo protection, in return for a tribute-paying Egbaland, which lacked the military organization that was capable of effectively protecting itself.[24] This tribute was eventually to become a yoke that the Egba sought to remove.

As we saw in the previous section, beyond winning independence for the Egba in 1774, Lisabi taught them how to effectively protect that freedom, especially against the fierce Dahomeans, who were also securing their freedom from Oyo. Lisabi further gave new laws to his people and taught them how to trade, not just in corn, but also in kola nuts and cloth to their best advantage. Jealous Ogboni chiefs are said to have presaged the downfall of Lisabi. They felt that the young men whom he conscripted into a standing army were better employed on the farms and arranged for his assassination during a Dahomean raid.[25]

The aftermath of Lisabi's demise saw Egbaland plunged into a series of four civil wars at the beginning of the 1820s until the larger Yoruba civil wars engulfed them in 1828.[26] It is ironical that Lisabi's own province of Ake should have been the most troubled at this time. Apparently, the people of Ake Province were the most truculent. Three of the four outbreaks of the war started in Ake Province and, in different ways, involved financial matters. The fourth war arose over chieftaincy rights at Ilugun in Oke-Ona Province.

The internecine wars among the Egba made them defenseless when attacked by the Ijebu and Ife during the Yoruba civil wars. The genesis of these attacks lies with the breakup of the Old Oyo Empire. From about 1796, one of the bulwarks of the empire, the strong central authority, began to diminish. An interregnum existed, which, because of the resultant administrative collapse and insecurity to life and property, caused Oyo citizens to flee the town and royal princes to seek fiefdoms for themselves. The last of the civil wars was the most serious in its consequences for Yorubaland. This was the Owu War, which lasted from 1821 to 1828. The immediate cause was a quarrel between two traders over two cowrie shells' worth of guinea pepper. The remote cause was the kidnapping of Oyo subjects by the Ife for sale at their markets in Apomu. First one town, then another, became involved as mediators, then as participants. The unwritten constitution of Yorubaland decreed that no Ife town was to be invaded by other Yoruba towns. The Olowu, the Oba of Owu, decided to do just that when he invaded Apomu, an Ife town. This in spite of an ominous precedent when Alafin Awole had tried unsuccessfully to attack Apomu in 1793. Owu was the southern defender of the Oyo cause and was asked to take punitive measures against Apomu by the Onikoyi of Ikoyi and Toyeje of Ogbomosho for their own purposes. Owu saw itself as the harbinger of a new day for Yorubaland. Ife still supported the old constitution. Hence, with his traditional authority, the Oni, the Oba of Ife, ordered the total destruction of Owu. The Ijebu, and a large segment of Oyo's population, for their own reasons, took up the Oni's cause. Owu was eventually destroyed, although it put up a strong fight before capitulating. The Owu fled into Egba territory, where they were pursued. Being now involved, Egba towns were also raised to the ground, weakened as they were by their own series of wars. The Owu were not aided by the leadership of their northern instigators, the Oyo, because they were temporarily preoccupied with the Fulani Jihad of Usman dan Fodio and its attempts to enter Yorubaland. Hence the apparent weakness of such a powerful people as the Owu. The main aim of Fulani incursions into Yorubaland at this time was religious.

The Egba were now in total disarray. The only important Egba towns left standing were Ibadan, Ijaye, and Ilugun. This forced the Egba to found a new town at Abeokuta in 1830, whose predominant geographical features, a large rock and valley location, afforded them some relief from marauding armies.[27]

Following the Owu war in 1828, the Egba deserted their old homes and wandered across the River Ogun.[28] The first to arrive at Abeokuta was Liperu, an Ogboni chief who, as a war escapee, had crossed the River Ogun for fear of being recaptured. Realizing that he was now safe, he decided to build a home for himself. The first to join him were three hunters—Jibulu, Oso, and Olu-nle, who took up residence in the caves on the eastern side of the River Ogun. They described their home to acquaintances as being "under stone." Hence, when the town developed around the general area, it was known as Abeokuta, literally "under stone." These caves were part of the Olumo Rock, an outcrop of hills that provided natural and secure abodes for its inhabitants. The word "olumo" engenders variegated interpretations. One hermeneutical elucidation is that "olumo" is a contraction of *Oluwa mo*, meaning "built by the Lord." Once reportedly serving as a temple to the god of crocodiles, the rock is still so venerated as a source of civic pride that it has inspired its own anthem:

On the Hills and in the Valleys

(1) On the hills and in the valleys,
There I was born
There I was bred
And brought up
In an independent state.
I shall stand on the Olumo Rock
And rejoice in the name of Egbaland.
I am a descendant of Lisabi.

Chorus:
I shall rejoice, rejoice
And rejoice,
On the Olumo Rock,
Rejoice! Rejoice! O
Rejoice! On the Olumo Rock.

(2) Abeokuta, the land of
The Egba people,
I shall not forget thee,
I shall put thee foremost
In my heart,
As a Nigerian city
I shall rejoice on the Olumo Rock,
I shall boast of this
In my heart,
That in a foremost town
There live the Egba people.

Chorus:
I shall rejoice, rejoice
And rejoice,
On the Olumo Rock,
Rejoice! Rejoice! O
Rejoice! On the Olumo Rock.[29]

In Yoruba, the first verse of the Egba National Anthem may be rendered thus:

(1) Lori oke ati petele
Ni be la gbe bi mi o
Ni be la gbe to mi dagba o
Ile ominira
Emi o f' Abeokuta s'ogo
N oduro lori Olumo
Ma yo loruko Egba o
Emi omo Lisabi[30]

An alternative name for Abeokuta was Oko Adagba (Adagba's village), after an early warrior who became famous as a brave defender of the new settlement. The town has outlived Adagba's exploits.[31] Liperu established the viability of the new town of Abeokuta by divination of the Ifa Oracle, and it began to grow, mainly under Oba Sodeke. Here, the Egba reorganized, dividing the town into three sections just as in the Egba forests, their homeland. A fourth section, Owu, was added in the southwest, between 1834 and 1835, as the Olowu and people of the old Owu kingdom came to join the Egba in their new municipal endeavors.[32]

In the original homeland, the governmental structure of the Egba was double-tiered. Each province of the federation had a predominant Oba and a council made up of chiefs. The dual partnership in government between the Oba and the elite of the Ogboni, Parakoyi, and Ologun was carried forward from the homeland to the new settlement at Abeokuta. Here, however, the Alake would gain acceptance as the spokesperson for the city-state. The Ogboni would also gain in importance. Conflicts in government were based on personalities and the perception of the common good. Class and religion were not important factors in political disputes.

The first forty years of Abeokuta's existence saw the town engaged in the tripartite struggle for succession to the Old Oyo Empire. Indeed, the town had been founded by a group of Egba led by Sodeke of Iporo (known by his military title of Seriki). They left Ibadan, where they had become unwelcomed, and joined a small group of Egba hunters living at the site of Abeokuta. Ibadan and Ijaye, the other two strong Yoruba towns, tried to form small empires of their own and vied with Abeokuta for Yoruba paramountcy following the decline and fall of Old Oyo. During this period, the Ologun were the real authority in Abeokuta, overshadowing the Ogboni as the highest authority. The position of the Alake for the whole city-state was not yet definitive. Once an Alake emerged as the *primus inter pares* ruler amongst the Egba, Prince Olusunmade Akin-Olugbade of Owu recently reiterated to the author that a further Anglophone method of distinguishing amongst the Obas used to be through the appellation of "His Royal Majesty" to characterize the Alake, while the other Obas were referred to as "His Royal Highness." This distinction is no longer the case, as many formerly subordinate Obas have now been elevated to primary status. When the question of succession to the imperial prestige of Old Oyo had been settled in favor of Ibadan, the Ologun in Abeokuta still retained their importance, as Abeokuta became the western defender of Yorubaland against the bellicose designs of Dahomey. Attacks by Dahomey lasted from 1844 to 1864. In 1854, Okukenu emerged as the first Alake of Egbaland who would try to offset the administrative weaknesses of a federal Abeokuta by being *nulli secundus* in Egbaland.

The British in Nigeria and the Arrival of the Saro

We have traced sketchily the development of Egbaland from its beginnings to the middle of the nineteenth century. Before proceeding with our narrative, it is necessary to consider the origins of British influence in Egbaland. The British are important in Egba history, not only for the establishment of a colonial administration and the consequent granting of independence to Nigeria, but also for the introduction of Christianity and literacy to Abeokuta.

In 1787, the African Association was founded in England in order to explore the course of the River Niger.[33] This was because the British were literally in the dark about the hinterland of any part of Africa. Consequently, in Nigeria, explorers such as Mungo Park explored the course of the River Niger. In the 1820s, Clapperton and Denham approached Nigeria from North Africa. In the 1830s, Richard and John Lander discovered that the River Niger actually formed a freshet into the Atlantic Ocean via its confluence with the Benue River. This information had not been divulged voluntarily to Europeans by prospective Nigerians. The rivers Niger and Benue now form the most distinguishing geographical features of modern Nigeria.

The explorations to acquire scientific knowledge about Africa, and specifically Nigeria, were not completely altruistic in that they served as the precursors for exploiting the people of the hinterland, both politically and religiously. Some indigenous rulers, such as the alafin of Oyo, welcomed the British as potential political allies while other monarchs, such as the Oba of Lagos, were chary of the motivations of the neophyte immigrants.

Concomitant with further explorations of the hinterland were efforts to abolish the slave trade. Between 1492 and about 1870, approximately eleven million Africans were carried as slaves to one part or another of the Americas. At the height of the traffic in the 1780s, the British and French each carried nearly forty thousand slaves a year. As early as 1755, Jean-Jacques Rousseau in his *Discours sur l'origine et les fondements de l'inegalite*, condemned slavery "as the final manifestation of the degrading and idiotic principle of authority."[34]

In England, a prince from modern-day Ghana, William Ansah Sessaracoa made an impact on high society as the embodiment of the "noble negro."

Although this pictorial ignored the inhumane treatment of ordinary Africans, the romanticism served its purpose. By the time Sessaracoa returned to the Gold Coast in 1752, "the combination of popular poetry and of journalism was beginning to have its desired effect on cultivated imaginations in England and in North America on the subject of slavery . . . The relative freedom of expression in Britain explains why, despite the imaginative force with which French philosophers wrote, 'abolitionism' prospered first in the Anglo-Saxon countries."[35]

The concept of abolitionism received its necessary tenacity of purpose when it attracted the oratory of William Wilberforce, who first introduced an antislavery bill in the English House of Commons on May 12, 1789.[36] In 1804, on his fourth attempt, Wilberforce's parliamentary efforts actually succeeded when a bill against the slave trade passed in the English House of Commons by forty-nine votes to twenty-four.[37] Finally, Wilberforce had overcome all trenchant opposition, and his herculean task of securing abolitionist legislation reached its fruition by receiving royal approbation. The slave trade was declared illegal as of May 1, 1807.[38]

Protestant and Catholic organizations were also at the vanguard of the abolitionist movement as they argued that Christianity would help to eradicate the slave trade. Manumitted slaves would be converted to Christianity and engage in legitimate trade as well as serve to counter the potency of Islam, which was also being proselytized in Nigeria at this time. Beginning in the 1830s, many emancipated slaves, such as Samuel Ajayi Crowther, were repatriated to Nigeria from Sierra Leone to promulgate the concept of the "bible and the plough."

British presence in Yorubaland owes its development to the policies of Lord Palmerston as the British secretary of state for foreign affairs. In 1849, James Beecroft was appointed as consul for the Bights of Benin and Biafra, residing at Fernando Po.[39] This was a first step toward colonization, taken within twenty years of the establishment of Abeokuta. Palmerston resolved to suppress the slave trade in the Bight of Benin. The first point of attack was Lagos. Kosoko, then Oba of Lagos, was an ardent slaver who had driven out his mild-mannered uncle, King Akitoye. Under Abeokutan sponsorship and British military aid, Akitoye was restored to the throne on Christmas Eve of 1851 in return for the stoppage of the slave trade. Thus was formed an official alliance between the British in Lagos and the Egba in Abeokuta. This friendship was quickly tested when a few years later, the Egba successfully appealed to Consul Campbell in Lagos for military help in repelling yet another raid by Dahomey.

The British consular period in Lagos lasted for only ten years. In 1861, Lagos was annexed as a colony. Between 1861 and 1893, the policies and preoccupations of the British administration quickly became established as the development of legitimate trade, especially that of palm produce, "with the consequential emphasis on the opening of the interior and the maintenance of free and secure movement on the roads."[40] Despite the 1865 British Parliamentary Select Committee's recommendations to the contrary, this policy was aggressively followed by Governor Glover. Glover's policies threatened to bypass Abeokuta, which set up customs posts to forestall this eventuality. Glover, suspicious of Abeokuta's attempts to extend its influence into his colony, declared that Ebute-Metta, an erstwhile Abeokuta town, was Lagos territory. This precipitated an armed insurrection in 1867 against all Europeans in Abeokuta—the incident known as *ifole* (housebreaking).[41]

British government officials were not the only British nationals who were active in West Africa at this time. In Yorubaland, as in almost everywhere else in West Africa, the Bible preceded the scepter. The first permanent Christian mission was established in Abeokuta in 1846 by the Church Missionary Society of England (CMS). The first converts were Sarah Ibikotan and her son, Adesina; Efutike, the wife of Chief Okukenu, the first Alake of Abeokuta; and Hannah Afala, Bishop Ajayi Crowther's mother. The first baptism was held in Ake on February 5, 1848.[42] The Methodists followed the CMS in 1847. The American Baptist Mission was established in 1850 while the Roman Catholics did not arrive in Abeokuta until 1885. From the 1850s onward, missionaries became a force in Abeokutan politics. In 1851, when the city of Abeokuta was attacked by Dahomey in retaliation for heavy losses suffered in a previous battle, European missionaries greatly helped to repel the attack.[43] It was the Anglican missionary Reverend Townsend who, in 1854, persuaded the Egba chiefs to end the interregnum and elect a successor to Regent Somoye by crowning Oba Okukenu as the Alake of Abeokuta and thus form a unitary government.[44] Many of the Egba became Christians.[45]

Missionaries of all persuasions, but especially those of the CMS, sought a close affiliation with Lagos. This was because of the protection afforded them by the presence there, starting in 1851, of the British government.

As a result of this missionary push, Abeokuta became just another one of the circumjacent territories of Lagos in a political, as well as a geographical, sense. This protection soon turned into a yoke for the missionaries. Both they and the African population sought their freedom. Independence from this protection came in 1893, when England granted Abeokuta a special status of home rule within the burgeoning British territory of Nigeria. It was to last until 1914 when the geographical expression that is Nigeria came into being.

Why was Abeokuta singled out for this special treatment by the British? The missionary presence that we have delineated in Abeokuta was felt in other towns in Nigeria also, so that was not the only reason. What marked Abeokuta out as being special was the proportionately large number and influence of repatriates from Sierra Leone (the Saro) and Brazil (the Amaro). Sierra Leone in the nineteenth century was populated by liberated slaves from different parts of Africa who had been retaken by British cruisers of the British Preventive Squadron in the Atlantic Ocean and landed in Sierra Leone. Many Yoruba-speaking liberated slaves returned to the Slave Coast, especially around Lagos, as part of the British repatriation movement to evangelize the west coast of Africa. Since most were Egba, and since they were at first unwelcome in Lagos by the slavers, the emancipated slaves moved to Abeokuta, which was enjoying a period of peace under Oba Sodeke, their paramount monarch.[46] They later shifted back to Lagos. This migration into Abeokuta started around 1840 and preceded the cession of Lagos. Indeed, it was the Saro Samuel Ajayi Crowther who was sent to London to persuade the British that it was in their interest to in fact cede Lagos and foster legitimate trade under Akitoye, the legitimate Oba of Lagos.[47]

In addition to the Saro in Abeokuta, there were manumitted African slaves who had acquired their freedom in Brazil and had gradually made their way back to Abeokuta. Not as numerous as the Saro, these repatriates were known as the Amaro. Some of the architecture in Lagos today bears evidence of their presence and influence in Nigeria. They were different from the Saro in that, having endured slavery, they were much more servile in attitude and comportment toward the British whom they encountered in Lagos and Abeokuta.

The Saro, much more so than the Amaro, were disliked by other Yoruba for their haughtiness. Since the Saro did not voluntarily wish to antagonize those whom they met upon arrival in Yorubaland, many of them sought to melt into the culture by becoming Ogboni and indistinguishable from other Egba. However, very few succeeded. We are concerned primarily with those Saro and Amaro who, although of Egba ancestry, upon returning to Abeokuta, formed a separate entity within the town. They were Christian for the most part. Many were traders, tailors, clerks, or teachers. All spoke English, had English names, and, in time, formed an oligarchy in the government of Abeokuta: they were a veritable new elite. They worked closely with the missionaries in both evangelizing and trying to retain Abeokuta's separate identity from British rule. Due partly to their efforts, Abeokuta became an example of true indirect rule under British hegemony. The British agreed not to occupy Abeokuta when, as from 1892, they began to actively acquire territoriality in southern Nigeria. This fact is the first contributory factor in making Abeokuta unique among the local government bodies of western Nigeria. No other town in Nigeria was ever accorded this treatment. Even the northern towns were occupied, although the British agreed not to interfere with the religion of the people. Abeokuta's position was a reward for the "civilizing" and missionary zeal that it had shown itself capable of, due in part to the new elite. This point is important because it clearly enabled Abeokuta to grow administratively as it wished.

We have identified the various levels of government in Abeokuta prior to the period under delineation. Indigenously, there were the institutions of the Alake and the elite made up of the Ogboni, the Ologun, and the Parakoyi. These ruled over the people with the help of assorted groups of age grades, associations, and trade organizations. Added to these was the level of the new elite of the Saro and the Amaro. They were separate from, and at times equal to, both the Alake and the elite. As the Saro sought a position in government for themselves, they oscillated between cooperation with, and subversion of, traditional authority.

The Impact of the British on the Egba

After 1861, a British colonial government was superimposed over Abeokuta's indigenous administration. The government was aided in a very real sense, and in a more or less consistent manner, by the evangelizing missionary. In 1892-93, all the Yoruba states, except Abeokuta, lost their separate identities as political units. They were brought under British control as a protectorate, administered with the colony of Lagos, from Lagos. Abeokuta retained an anomalous self-independence. In 1906, the colony and protectorate in

Yorubaland were extended and amalgamated with the Niger Coast (formerly Oil Rivers) protectorate farther east, to form the protectorate of southern Nigeria. In 1914, Nigeria was born, as the protectorates of southern and northern Nigeria were amalgamated into a single unit. In this structure, Abeokuta's self-government was terminated. It too was ruled directly by the British, although with an indigenous governmental body.

From 1906, when Sir Frederick Lugard published *Native Administration* and popularized the expression of "indirect rule" in Nigeria, to 1960, when Nigeria gained its independence, Nigeria was governed under the indirect-rule system as propagated by Lugard. This expediency of ruling indirectly through established chiefs as a mechanism for accomplishing political evolution recognized the inadequacy of British staffing that Lugard had to govern under. The organizing principles of local self-government utilized by the indirect-rule system were extended from India primarily because there were no perceived reasons why they should not pertain to Nigeria. The linchpin of the three originating conceptualizations of the indirect-rule policy was the second one in which Lugard opined that "every advanced community should be given the widest possible powers of self-government under its own ruler, and that these powers should be rapidly increased with the object of complete independence at the earliest possible date in the not distant future."[48]

Ratification of the legitimacy of indigenous chiefs, wherever their powers were first evident, initially in northern Nigeria and later throughout Nigeria, was cemented by several ordinances such as the *Native Authority Ordinance*, which invested a chief with political power over all indigenes resident in his area; the *Native Courts Ordinance*, which reinforced indigenous laws and customs; and the *Native Revenue Ordinance*, which identified a chief as the fiat with fiduciary powers.[49]

Once ensconced as a native authority, the fortunes of a chief turned as much on the capriciousness of British officials who were loathe to immix their powers, as it did on the allometric and allopatric characteristics of the indirect-rule system itself. Its very vertiginousness made the practice of indirect rule an omnibus, though revered, policy with spotty successes in Nigeria as elsewhere.

During its "independence," Abeokuta experimented with a new government (the Egba United Government), instituted electrical and water works, and attempted to broaden the tax base for its rather overburdened bureaucracy. An independent Abeokuta, however, was not to be. Lugard, in 1914, used the opportunity of a weak government in Abeokuta, and local unrest, to demand the surrender of its independence. He did not want any pockets of self-government in the Protectorate of Nigeria as this would undermine his power and importance. The brief interlude of independence provided Abeokuta with a unique experience in self-government during the British era. After 1914, the electrical-streetlights project in Abeokuta was cancelled, and the water works became inoperable.[50]

The British rule in Nigeria from 1849 to 1861 was headed by a consul. After 1861, the informal position of a consul was upgraded to that of a governor at the center in Lagos.[51] The apparatus of government was embellished by a travelling commissioner for each protectorate. He was a liaison officer between the provinces and the center. Next in the hierarchy was the resident, in charge of a group of provinces within a protectorate. Then came "the man on the spot," the district officer, who was in every major town to oversee the day-to-day running of the British Empire. In 1939, the travelling commissioner became known as the chief commissioner with similar duties.[52] In that year, Nigeria was divided up into three provinces, namely the northern, eastern, and western provinces, with a regional authority for each province. The chief commissioner was directly responsible to the governor in Lagos, who in turn reported to the foreign secretary at the colonial office in Whitehall. In 1952, the cognomen "Provinces" was changed to "Regions" to identify Nigeria's political divisions consequent to the new Nigerian constitution of 1951 (refer to appendix C of the 1951 constitution). The name was retained until the creation of states in 1967 (refer to appendix C of the 1951 constitution) when the states were totally run by Nigerians. Prior to independence in 1960, the government structure that emerged in western Nigeria was that of an indigenous local government authority consisting of an Oba and his chiefs closely monitored by a British regional authority made up of a chief commissioner, residents, and district officers.

In this chapter, we have described the ethnography of the Yoruba, and defined how the Yoruba were affected by the advent of the British. Particular attention was paid to the Egba, the ethnicity within the Yoruba with which we are most directly concerned. Being forced to move from their original homeland to a central location at Abeokuta because of civil war, the Egba then vied for a position for themselves among the other ethnicities that make up the generic term "Yoruba." From the 1840s, a group of repatriated manumitted slaves began to make their presence felt on the local scene.[53] We have described the arrival of the Saro. The arrival of the British added to the local political picture at about this time. Gradually, the British acquired the trappings of a colonial administration with a governor at the center in Lagos and a regional government in the provinces of Nigeria. In Abeokuta, this British administration was superimposed over an indigenous government made up of the Alake, the elite, and a new elite of the repatriated émigrés. Britain's impact on Abeokuta was felt through the imposition of an alien government and the introduction of Christianity and literacy.

In the following chapter, we will illustrate how the new elite of the Saro sought a governmental role for themselves in Abeokuta. This led to the creation of two new government structures that were as much a product of the enculturation as it was the acculturation of the Saro. The chapter will also focus on Alake Ademola II. His character was of utmost importance in the shifts of government during the period under study. The Alake's first attempt at restructuring the government of Abeokuta will be examined.

SUGGESTIONS FOR FURTHER READING

Abraham, Roy Cline. *Dictionary of Modern Yoruba*. London: University of London Press, 1958.

Adeyemo, Bade. *Yoruba as a Language of an Immediate Environment*. Abeokuta, Nigeria: GOAD Education Publisher, 1998.

Adejuyigbe, O. *Boundary Problems in Western Nigeria: A Geographical Analysis*. Ile-Ife: University Ife Press, 1973.

————, and Michael Crowder, eds. *History of West Africa*. 3rd ed. (2 volumes). London: Longman, 1988.

Adetubgo, Abiodun. *The Yoruba Language in Western Nigeria: Its Major Dialect Areas*. New York: Columbia University (thesis) 1967.

Adewale, Lawrence Olufemi. *The Yoruba Language: Published Works and Doctoral Dissertations, 1843-1986*. Hamburg: Buske, 1987.

Ajisafe, Ajayi Kolawole. *The Laws and Customs of the Yoruba People*. Lagos: Kash & Klare Bookshop, 1946

————. *History of Abeokuta*. Lagos: Kash & Klare Bookshop, 1948.

Akintoye, S. Adebanji. *A History of the Yoruba People*. Melksham; Amalion Publishing, 2010.

Alie, Joe A. *A New History of Sierra Leone*. New York: Saint Martin's Press, 1990.

Amadi, E. *Ethics in Nigerian Culture*. Ibadan: Heinemann Educational Books, 1982.

Armstrong, Robert G. *Yoruba Numerals*. Ibadan: Oxford University Press, published for the Nigerian Institute of Social and Economic Research, 1962.

Asiwaju, A. I. *Partitioned Africans: Ethnic Relations across Africa's International Boundaries, 1884-1984*. London: C. Hurst, 1985.

Awe, Bolanle, ed. *Nigerian Women in Historical Perspective*. Lagos: Sankore Publishers, 1992.

Bamgbose, Ayo. *Yoruba Orthography: A Linguistic Appraisal with Suggestions for Reform*. Ibadan: Ibadan University Press, 1965.

————. *A Grammar of Yoruba*. Cambridge: University Press in association with the West African Languages Survey and the institute of African Studies, Ibadan, 1966.

————. *A Short Yoruba Grammar*. Ibadan; London: Heinemann, 1967.

————. *Yoruba, a Language in Transition*. Yaba, Lagos: J. F. Odunjo Memorial Lectures, 1986.

Barber, Karin. "How Man Made God in West Africa: Yoruba Attitudes Towards the Orisa," *Africa 51*, 1981.

Barnes, Sandra T., ed. *Africa's Ogun: Old World and New*. Bloomington: Indiana University Press, 1997.

Biobaku, Saburi O. *The Egba and Their Neighbours, 1842-1872*. London: Oxford University Press, 1957.

Bovill, E. W. *Missions to the Niger*. London: Hakluyt, 1996.

Bowen, T. J. *Grammar and Dictionary of the Yoruba Language, with an Introductory Description of the Country and People of Yoruba*. Washington: Smithsonian Institution, 1958.

Burton, Richard Francis. *Wit and Wisdom from West Africa: A Book of Proverbial Philosophy, Idioms, Enigmas, and Laconisms*. London: Biblo-Moser, 1969.

Courtenay, Karen Ruth. *A Generative Phonology of Yoruba*. Los Angeles: University of California. PhD thesis, 1968.

Crowder, Michael. *West Africa under Colonial Rule*. London: Hutchinson, 1968.

―――. *The Story of Nigeria, 1978.*

―――. *West African Resistance: The Military Response to Colonial Occupation*. rev. ed. Revised Edition, 1978.

Crowther, Samuel Adjai. *A Vocabulary of the Yoruba Language*. London: Church Missionary Society, 1870.

Curtin, Phillip, Steven Feierman, Leonard Thompson, and Jan Vansina. *African History, 1978.*

Digest of Local Government Statistics. Abeokuta: Ogun State of Nigeria: Ministry of Finance and Economic Planning, Central Department of Statistics, 1989.

Fabunmi, M. A. *Yoruba Idioms*. 'Wande Abimbola, ed. Lagos: Pilgrim Books, 1969.

Falola, Toyin and Biodun Adediran. *Islam and Christianity in West Africa*. Ile-Ife: University of Ife Press, 1983.

―――. 1984. *The Political Economy of a Pre-colonial African State, Ibadan, ca. 1830-1900*. Ile-Ife: University of Ife Press, 1984.

―――, and Biodun Adediran, eds. 1986. *Nigeria before 1800 A.D.* Lagos: John West, 1986.

―――, ed. *Britain and Nigeria: Exploitation or Development?* London: Zed Books, 1987.

―――, et al. *History of Nigeria: Before A.D. 1800s. Vol 1* Lagos: Longman, 1989.

Flint, John. *Sir George Goldie and the Making of Nigeria*. London: Oxford University Press, 1960.

Gailey, Harry Alfred. *Lugard and the Abeokuta Uprising: The Demise of Egba Independence*. London; Totowa, NJ: F. Cass, 1982.

Hafkin, Nancy, and Edna Bay, eds. *Women in Africa, 1976*.

Hodgkin, T. *Nigerian Perspectives: An Historical Anthology*. London: Oxford University Press, 1975.

Idowu, E. B. *Olodumare: God in Yoruba Belief*. London: Longman, 1962.

Ikime, O. *The Fall of Nigeria: The British Conquest*. London: Heinemann, 1977.

Isichei, Elizabeth. *A History of Christianity in Africa: From Antiquity to the Present*. Grand Rapids, MI: Eerdsmans, 1995.

Kalu, O. U. *Divided People of God: Church Union Movement in Nigeria, 1875-1966*. New York: Nok Publishers, 1978.

———. *Christianity in West Africa: The Nigerian Story*. Ibadan: Day Star Press, 1978.

———. *The History of Christianity in West Africa*. London: Longman, 1980.

Kastfelt, Niels. *Religion and Politics in Nigeria: A Study in Middle Belt Christianity*. New York: Saint Martin's Press, 1994.

Kukah, Mathews Hassan, and Toyin Falola. *Religious Militancy and Self-Assertion: Islam and Politics in Nigeria*. London: Avebury, 1996.

Losi, J. B. Ogunjimi. *History of Abeokuta*. Lagos: Bosere Press, 1924.

Lugard, F. *The Dual Mandate in British Tropical Africa*. London: Frank Cass, 1922.

Mazrui, Ali. *The Africans: A Triple Heritage, 1986*.

Mbiti, J. S. *African Religions and Philosophies*. New York: Praeger, 1970.

McCarthy, Stephen. *Africa: The Challenge of Transformation, 1994*.

Miers, Suzanne and Martin A. Klein. *Slavery and Colonial Rule in Africa*. Portland, OR: Frank Cass Publishers, 1999.

Nicolson, I. F. *The Administration of Nigeria 1900-1960: Men, Methods and Myths*. Oxford: Clarendon Press, 1975.

Nwauna, Apollos O. "State Formation in Africa: A Reconsideration of the Traditional Theories," *Africa Quarterly*, vol. 27, nos. 3-4, 1988-89.

————. "The Europeans in Africa: Prelude to Colonialism," *African History and Cultures to 1885*. Toyin Falola, ed. Durham, Florida: Carolina Academic Press, 2000.

Peel, John David Yeadon. *Aladura: A Religious Movement among the Yoruba*. London: Oxford University Press for International African Institute, 1968.

Perham, M. *Lugard*. London: Collins, 1960.

Rodney, Walter. *How Europe Underdeveloped Africa*. Wahington, D.C.: Howard University Press, 1981.

Sanneh, Lamin. *The Crown and the Turban: Muslims and West African Pluralism*. Boulder, CO: Westview, 1997.

Smith, Robert S. *Kingdoms of the Yoruba*. 3rd edition. Madison: University of Wisconsin Press, 1988.

Spencer, J. *A History of Islam in West Africa*. Oxford: Oxford University Press, 1970.

Sundkler, Bengt and Christopher Steed. *A History of the Christian Church in Afric*a. New York: Cambridge University Press, 1999.

Tumano, Tekena N. *The Evolution of the Nigerian State: The Southern Phase, 1898-1914*. London: Longman, 1972.

Usman, Yusufu Bala, ed. *Studies in the History of the Sokoto Caliphate*. Zaria, Nigeria: Ahmadu Bello University Press, 1979.

Vogel, Joseph O., ed. *The Encyclopedia of Precolonial Africa: Archaeology, History, Languages, Cultures, and Environment*. Walnut Creek, CA: AltaMira Press, 1997.

Williams, Pat., and Toyin Falola. *Religious Impact on the Nation State: The Nigerian Predicament*. London: Avebury, 1995.

Young, C. *The African Colonial State in Comparative Perspectives*. New Haven: Yale University Press, 1994.

Zachernuk, Philip S. *Colonial Subjects: An African Intelligensia and Atlantic Ideas*. Charlottesville: University Press of Virginia, 2000.

INTERNET RESOURCES

The following Internet sites contain written and visual materials that are germane to this chapter.

Biography of Alake Ademola II of Abeokuta
<http://www.africaexpert.org/people/profiles/profilesforperson4231.html>
Retrieved December 3, 2002

<http://en.wikipedia.org/wiki/User:King_of_Abeokuta>
Retrieved September 18, 2009

Chronology of the Alakes of Abeokuta
<http://www.worldstatesmen.org/Nigeria_native.html>
Retrieved July 29, 2003

Colonialism and the Culture of Non-European Cultures
<http://www.scholars.nus.edu.sg/landow/post/nigeria/yourbavic.html>
Retrieved February 26, 2003

Indigo dye pits at Kofar Mata as examples of the dyeing process (Hausa Institute, Bayero University, Kano)
<http://home.att.net/~amanders/nigeria/>
Retrieved April 20, 2003

History of Nigeria
<http://countryreports.org/history/nigehist.htm>
Retrieved February 26, 2003

History of Sierra Leone
<http://www.africast.com/country_history.php?strCountry=Sierra%20Leone>
Retrieved February 26, 2003

Nigeria
<http://lcweb2.loc.gov/cgi-bin/query/r?frd/cstdy:@field(DOCID+ng0015)>
Retrieved February 26, 2003

Nigeria: Abolition of the Slave Trade
    <http://lcweb2.loc.gov/cgi-bin/query/r?frd/cstdy:@field(DOCID+ng0023)>
    Retrieved February 26, 2003

Nigeria: The Yoruba Wars
    <http://lcweb2.loc.gov/cgi-bin/query/r?frd/cstdy:@field(DOCID+ng0022)>
    Retrieved February 26, 2003

Nigeria: Usman dan Fodio and the Sokoto Caliphate
    <http://lcweb2.loc.gov/cgi-bin/query/r?frd/cstdy:@field(DOCID+ng0021)>
    Retrieved February 26, 2003

Nigerian Literature: Oral and Written Traditions
    <http://www.scholars.nus.edu.sg/landow/post/nigeria/orality.html>
    Retrieved February 26, 2003

Perspectives on Africa
    <http://www.africaresource.com>
    Retrieved June 21, 2003

The Correct History of Edo
    *<http://lw14fd.law14.hotmail.msn.com/cgi-bin/getmsg?curmbox=F00000
    0001&a=d943508 . . . >*
    Retrieved January 15, 2003

The Effect of Colonialism on the Oba
    <http://www.scholars.nus.edu.sg/landow/post/nigeria/oba.html>
    Retrieved February 26, 2003

END NOTES

1. Saburi O. Biobaku. *The Egba and Their Neighbours, 1842-1872*. London: Oxford University Press, 1957: p.17

2. S. O. Biobaku. *The Egba and Their Neighbours, 1842-1872:* pp.1-2; also, Rev. Samuel Johnson. *The History of the Yorubas*. London: Lowe & Brydone, 1921: pp. 3-8; also, S. Adebanji Akintoye. *A History of the Yoruba People*. Melksham: Amalion Publishing, 2010.

3. P. A. Talbot. *The People of Southern Nigeria*. London: Oxford University Press, 1926: pp. 276-278; also, I. A. Akinjogbin. "Origin and History of the Yoruba," in *An Introduction to Western Nigeria: Its People, Culture and System of Government*, ed., Adebayo Adedeji, London: Hutchinson, 1968: p.10.

4. Oyeronke Oyewumi. "Conceptualizing Gender: The Eurocentric Foundations of Feminist Concepts and the Challenge of African Epistemologies." *Jenda: A Journal of Culture and African Women Studies*: 2, 1, 2002.

5. W. L. Avery, "Concepts of God in Africa." *Journal of the American Academy of Religion*, vol. 39, no. 3, 1971: p. 391.

6. S. A. Adewale. *The Religion of the Yoruba: A Phenomenological Analysis*. Ibadan, Nigeria: Department of Religious Studies, University of Ibadan, 1988. See also Fagunwa, D. O. *Adiitu Olodumare, pelu opolopo ibere*. Lagos: Nelson, 1964. The difference between Olorun and Olodumare (God) is one of usage by modernists and traditionalists.

7. J. Omosade Awolalu. *Yoruba Beliefs and Sacrificial Rites*. New York: Athelia Henrietta Press.

8. 'Wande Abimbola, and Barry Hallen. "Secrecy and Objectivity in the Methodology and Literature of Ifa Divination," in P. Nooter (ed.) *Secrecy: African Art that Conceals and Reveals*. New York: The Museum for African Art and Munich: Prestel, pp. 213-221. See also Robert G. Armstrong, tr. *Iyere Ifa = The deep chants of Ifa*. Ibadan: Institute of African Studies. University of Ibadan, 1978. Writing in *Ifa: An Exposition of Ifa Literary Corpus* (page 3), Abimbola

asserts that "the fact borne out of my research, however, is that the two names, Ifa and Orunmila, refer to the same deity. But while the name 'Orunmila' refers exclusively to the deity himself, the name 'Ifa' refers both to the deity and his divination system. Most Ifa priests interviewed by me maintained this point."

9.   S. O. Biobaku. *The Egba and Their Neighbours, 1842-1872, 1957:* p. 25.

10.   Toyin Falola. *Culture and Customs of Nigeria.* Westport, Connecticut: Greenwood Press, 2001: p. 35

11.   'Wande Abimbola. 1997. *Ifa: An Exposition of Ifa Literary Corpus.* New York: Athelia Henrietta Press, p.162.

12.   A. L. Mabogunje. *Urbanization in Nigeria.* London: University of London Press, 1968: p.95.

13.   The succession of Alakes is as follows:

Lisabi:	Liberator of the Egba, 1774-1819
Liperu:	Founder of Abeokuta, 1830
Sodeke:	Chief of Abeokuta, 1829-1845 (died 1845)
Somoye:	Regent of Abeokuta, 1845-1846 and 1862-1868
Okukenu:	Regent of Abeokuta, 1846-1854, as the *Sagbua*
	First Alake of Abeokuta, 8/8/1854-9/1/1862
Ademola I:	Second Alake of Abeokuta, 11/20/1869-12/30/1877
Oyekan:	Third Alake of Abeokuta, 1/18/1879-9/18/1881 (died 1881)
Oluwaji:	Fourth Alake of Abeokuta, 2/9/1885-1/27/1889
Sokalu:	Fifth Alake of Abeokuta, 9/18/1891-6/11/1898
Gbadebo I:	Sixth Alake of Abeokuta, 8/8/1898-5/28/1920
	Paramount ruler of Egbaland, circa 1914-5/28/1920

Sir Ladapo Samuel Ademola II:

> Seventh Alake of Abeokuta, 9/27/1920-7/29/1948 and 12/3/1950-12/27/1962
> Senior member of the Western Region Conference of Chiefs
> Knight of the British Empire (KBE), 1935; Companion of the Order of St. Michael and St. George (CMG); and Commander of the Order of the British Empire (CBE)
> Born: 9/20/1872
> Died: 12/27/1962

Adesina Samuel Gbadebo II:
>Eighth Alake of Abeokuta
>Paramount ruler of Egbaland 9/29/1963-1971

Michael Mofolorunso Oyebade Lipede:
>Ninth Alake of Abeokuta and paramount ruler of
>Egbaland since 8/5/1972
>Born: 1/26/1915
>Died: 2/3/2005

Michael Adedotun Aremu Gbadebo III:
>Tenth and regnant Alake of Abeokuta

14. In the *History of Abeokuta*, pp. 60-61, Ajisafe maintains that in the early days prior to the elevation of Okukenu as the first Alake,

> the position of a king was that of a nominal ruler; hence no care was taken in the choice of a king from a true royal blood.

> As a matter of fact, and with the exception of Gbagura dynasty, [sic] there has never existed a distinct royal family amongst the Egbas. Any one may be elected by divination from any of the Egba townships. There were times when an Itoku man, Ijemo and an Ijeun man respectively became the Alake by divination.

> Oba Okukenu himself was "of no Royal blood. By virtue of his being the oldest man in the house of the late Chief Losi (brother of Jibodu, one of the kings) he was elected the Alake."

15. S. O. Biobaku. *The Egba and Their Neighbours, 1842-1872, 1957: pp. 1-2.*

16. S. O. Biobaku. "An Historical Sketch of Egba Traditional Authorities." *Africa.* (London) 1952: p. 23.

17. Earl Phillips. "The Egba at Abeokuta: Acculturation and Political Change, 1830-70," *Journal of African History* 10, 1969: p. II9; S. O. Biobaku, "An Historical Sketch of Egba Traditional Authorities," *Africa 22*, January, 1952: p. 35-49; Daryll Forde, *The Yoruba-Speaking People of South-West Nigeria*, London: International African Institute, 1951: p. 23; also R. E. Bennett, "The Ogboni and Other Secret Societies in Nigeria," *Journal of the African Society*, 16, October, 1916: pp. 16-29.

18. P. C. Lloyd. "Political and Social Structure," in *Sources of Yoruba History*, ed. S. O. Biobaku. Oxford: Clarendon Press, 1973: p. 211.

19. A. A. B. Aderibigbe. "People of Southern Nigeria," in *A Thousand Years of West African History*, eds. J. F. Ade Ajayi and Ian Espie. New York: Humanities Press, 1972: p. 193.

For a revisionist history of Benin in which the reviewer, Osahon, maintains that the foundation of Yorubaland was actually established by a Bini named Ekaladerhan and that the *Ifa* myth of creation draws significantly from Bini and Egyptian corpora, see Naiwa Osahon, *The Correct History of Edo*. <http:// lw14fd.law14.hotmail.msn.com/cgi_bin/getmsg?curmbox=F000000001&a= d943508> Retrieved January 15, 2003.

20. S. O. Biobaku. *The Egba and Their Neighbours, 1842-1872, 1957: p. 8.*

21. S. O. Biobaku. *The Egba and Their Neighbours, 1842-1872, 1957: p. 8.*

22. Adebisin Folarin. *Egba History: Life Review, 1829-1930*. Chicago: University of Chicago Press, 1969: p. 6.

23. Robert Smith. *Kingdoms of the Yoruba*. London: Methuen Co., 1969: p. 82. Smith provided a succinct history of the early settlement of the Egba in Western Nigeria.

24. S. O. Biobaku. *The Egba and Their Neighbours, 1842-1872, 1957: p. 8.*

25. Robert Smith. *Kingdoms of the Yoruba:* p. 85.

26. Ajayi Ajisafe, *History of Abeokuta*, Lagos: Kash & Klare Bookshop, 1948: p. 29.

27. Reiteratively, Professor Biobaku avers that the year 1830 is the putative date of Liperu's arrival and settlement in Abeokuta. Indeed, the centenary of Abeokuta's establishment was officially celebrated in 1930. See also Patrick Ogunshakin, *Olumo*, p. 8.

28. The towns of Awe, Fiditi, Iloba, Abena, Akinmorin, Agerige Aran, Kojoku, and Oroko were not deserted; see Ajisafe, *History of Abeokuta:* p. 32; see also Curtin, *Africa Remembered*, pp. 318-321

29. Oladipo Odunoye, Olalekan Akinpelu, and 'Wale Ope-Agbe. *Oba Oyebade Lipede*. Lagos: Opeds Nigeria Limited, 1997: pp. 8-9.

30. Gabriel O. Olusanya. *Memoirs of a Disillusioned Patriot*. Ibadan, Nigeria: Helicon Press, p.12.

31. Ajisafe, *History of Abeokuta:* p.29, evinced that the more probable meaning of "olumo" is as a contraction of "olufimo," to designate the fact that the Egba had established a defensive settlement at which they fully intended to make a last stand, if need be, against their marauding enemies. The full quotation ascribed to the original settlers is *Oluwa fi gbogbo wahala wa mo. Olufimo, Olumo* (God put all our worries behind us)!

32. Jean H. Kopytoff. *A Preface to Modern Nigeria*. Milwaukee, WI: University of Wisconsin Press, 1965: pp. 16-17; also Adebisin Folarin, *Egba History: Life Review, 1829-1930:* p.12.

33. For this section, refer to Toyin Falola, *The History of Nigeria*, Westport: Greenwood Press, 1999: pp. 39-80.

34. Hugh Thomas. *The Slave Trade: The Story of the Atlantic Slave Trade, 1440-1870.* New York: Simon & Schuster, 1997: p. 466.

35. Hugh Thomas. *The Slave Trade,* 1997: p. 468.

36. Hugh Thomas. *The Slave Trade,* 1997: p. 513.

37. Hugh Thomas. *The Slave Trade,* 1997: p. 549.

38. Hugh Thomas. *The Slave Trade,* 1997: p. 556.

39. Sir William N. M. Geary. *Nigeria under British Rule*. New York: Barnes & Noble Inc. 1965: p.25.

40. Robert Smith. *Kingdoms of the Yoruba:* p. 171.

41. The *ifole* was an internal struggle among those in power in Abeokuta as to which faction, those for or against the British in Abeokuta, would gain authority. The pro-British, normally traditionalist forces, won the struggle for supremacy.

Ademola I became Alake in 1869 with the support of this faction. See, Phillips, *The Egba at Abeokuta*: p. 128-130.

42. Ajisafe. *History of Abeokuta*: p. 58.

43. Robert Smith. *Kingdoms of the Yoruba:* p. 166.

44. Robert Smith. *Kingdoms of the Yoruba:* p. 159.

45. Jean H. Kopytoff. *A Preface to Modern Nigeria*: p. 276.

46. William Geary. *Nigeria under British rule*: p. 30.

47. Robert Smith. *Kingdoms of the Yoruba*: p. 169.

48. A. H. M. Kirk-Greene. "1922: Lugard's Political Testimony." *The Principles of Native Administration in Nigeria, Selected Documents 1900-1947*. London: Oxford University Press, 1965, p. 153.

49. Amy M. McClure. *Local Governments in English-Speaking East and West Africa*, pp. 79-80, July 1968. Unpublished masters thesis, San Diego State College. San Diego, California, USA.

50. Agneta Pallinder-Law. "Aborted Modernization in West Africa? The case for Abeokuta," *Journal of African History*, 15, 1974: pp. 65-82. Other examples of arrested modernization are given as Bornu under Rabeh, the empires of Samori and Ahmadu Seku, Dahomey under Behanzin, Opobo under Jaja, the Yoruba city-states, especially Abeokuta and Ibadan, and the Accra and Fanti Confederacies of the Gold Coast.

51. The colonial governors during the period under study were the following: Lord Frederick Lugard, high commissioner of the Protectorate of Northern Nigeria (1900-1906), governor (1912-1914), governor-general (1914-1918); Sir Hugh Clifford, 1919-1925; Sir Bernard Bourdillon, 1935-1943; Sir Arthur Richards, 1943-1948; Sir John Macpherson, 1948-1954. For a short time during 1954, Sir John Richardson was governor-general of Nigeria. Refer to Michael Crowder, *A Short History of Nigeria*, p. 329.

52. The chief commissioners for the western provinces during the period under study were the following: G. G. Shute, CMG (acting chief commissioner, Southern Provinces) 1939; H. F. M. White (acting chief commissioner) 1939; G. C. Whitely, CMG, 1940-44; T. C. Hoskyns-Abrahall, CMG (acting chief commissioner) 1945; Sir Gerald C. Whitely, CMG, 1946-47; T. C. Hoskyns-Abrahall, CMG, 1948-51; H. F. Marshall, CMG (later lieutenant governor, Western Region) 1952.

53. Landmarks in the history of Abeokuta in the nineteenth and twentieth centuries, according to Ajisafe (A. K.), author of *History of Abeokuta*, 1964, revised edition, were the following:

1830 — Abeokuta established

1838 — Initial return of freed transatlantic slaves

1843 — Visit of Rev. Townsend

1845 — Oba Sodeke died

1845 — Movement to the present site of AKE township in Abeokuta

1846 — Christian Missionary Society (CMS) established in Abeokuta

1848 — Egba Obas write to Queen Victoria of England

1848 — Yoruba language reduced to writing

1849 — Queen Victoria's reply read to the Egba Obas

1849 — First corn mill worked in Abeokuta

1851 — First Dahomey invasion defeated

1854 — Oba Alake Gbadebo born

1854 — Oba Okukenu elected as the first Alake of Abeokuta

1855 — Oba Pawu elected as the first Olowu in Abeokuta

1857 — Expulsion of Madam Tinubu from Lagos

1859 — *Iwe irohin*, first newspaper in Nigeria, published

1862 — The Holy Bible first published in the Yoruba language

1863 — First brick molded in Abeokuta

1867 — Oba Ademola enthroned as the second Alake of Abeokuta (1869: see
   p. 53)

1887 — Madam Tinubu died

1893 — Treaty of Egba Independence signed with the British

1898 — Telegraph station opened at Lafenwa

1899 — Oba Karunwi, Osile of Oke-Ona, died

1901 — Vaccination introduced

1902 — A. Edun appointed as the secretary of the Egba United
   Government (EUG)

1903 — Sokori Bridge opened

1904 — Alake visited England and was received by King Edward VII

1908 — Abeokuta Grammar School founded

1908 — EUG Hospital founded

1909 — Corn-crushing machine established in Sapon

1910 — Oba Abolade enthroned as the Agura of Gbagura

1911 — Lanfewa Bridge opened

CHAPTER 3

THE EGBA SARO AND THE ALAKE AS INSTRUMENTS OF INSTITUTIONAL CHANGE IN ABEOKUTA

This chapter will describe in detail the political contributions made to Egba society by the new elite of the Saro and the Alake with whom they had to contend. As the Saro sought a governmental role for themselves in Abeokuta, they created two administrations in which they were dominant. These organizations were the Egba United Board of Management (EUBM) from 1865 to 1874 and the Egba United Government (EUG) from 1898 to 1914. We will examine these administrations that helped to fashion and advance Abeokuta's local government system. These administrations served the dual purposes of establishing the Saro in government as well as democratizing the personnel of that government. The dominant personalities among the Saro had to contend with another strong personality in Abeokuta during the period under study. This was Alake Ademola II. We will provide a biography of the Alake and indicate his contributions to Egba government.

The Egba United Board of Management, 1865-1874

Abeokuta's independence from direct British rule extended from 1898 to 1914 and formed a watershed for its new educated elite, the Saro.

Independence from Britain both confirmed the Saro's position and acted as a stimulus for their further governmental participation. The intelligentsia's systematic participation in Egba government started in 1865 under the aegis of the indirect-rule system, and not within an independent Abeokuta. The position of the new elite in government, as opposed to that of the traditional elite consisting of the Ogboni and Parakoyi, needs to be examined. Before 1939, the educated elite enjoyed two periods of sustained power. From 1865 to 1874, they controlled the Egba United Board of Management (EUBM) and, from 1898 to 1914, the Egba United Government (EUG). These two periods served as precedents for the participation in government of the educated elite between 1939 and 1952. There is an essential continuity of purpose on the part of the intelligentsia before and after 1939. It is this continuity in government by the Saro that helped to distinguish Abeokuta's administrative body as being the strongest, most viable local government entity in western Nigeria during the 1940s and 1950s.

What the educated elite yearned for was political and financial power.[1] Despite the fact that by 1855 the Egba Saro had carved out an important portion of the commercial-middleman function in Abeokuta for themselves, administrative employment was seen as a way toward further economic reward.[2] An obvious drawback to the smooth governing of Abeokuta before the 1860s was the number of people involved in its governmental process. This was calculated at some four thousand people in 1852, out of a population of one hundred thousand in midcentury.[3] The Egba had failed to modify the traditional methods of government in their homestead to meet the demands of their new environment at Abeokuta. It must be remembered, of course, that only thirty-six years had passed between the foundation of Abeokuta and the emergence of the Saro as a political force in that same town. However, because of the situation, the new elite saw a governmental role for themselves.[4] They would fashion a role for themselves by creating an advisory board for the Alake that would combine the authority of the traditional elite with the skills, ideas, and savvy of the "Westernized" Sierra Leonean repatriates. The advisory board was to be known as the Egba United Board of Management (EUBM).[5] It was to provide a much-needed central government for Abeokuta.[6] The resuscitated position of the Alake (in 1854) was still a weak institution. Shomoye, the Bashorun (traditional prime minister) of the Egba, was styled the president general of the board. However, the board was directed and controlled by its secretary, G. W. Johnson, and other leading Egba Saro traders and clerks—all members of the new elite.[7] Johnson was a former tailor and musician who returned to Lagos in 1863 and Abeokuta in 1865.[8] Professor Biobaku opined that the constitution of the EUBM remained obscure and that it did not show evidence of a proper council fully evolved to represent the traditional, sectional, and immigrant elements in Abeokuta.[9]

The board itself had three aims in mind to justify its existence. First, it would provide the town with a central executive. Next, it would provide the single voice that experience had shown was necessary in dealing with the British administration in Lagos. Thirdly, and equally as important, it would allow the Saro a forum in the political life of their adopted town, which was dominated by traditionalists.[10]

The Saro clearly could not stand by and allow the Alake alone to provide the single voice for Abeokuta in external affairs. In a word, the Saro, through the EUBM, wished to convert Abeokuta into "a Christian, civilized society,"[11] since they themselves were mostly Christians.

According to Professor Biobaku's lights,

> In fact the Board was little more than an empty bureaucracy, parading sovereign pretensions, and issuing largely idle threats. Its sole achievement was the establishment of a short-lived Customs Department for levying export duties instead of the customary tolls collected at the gates.[12]

In actuality, the board also succeeded in altering Abeokuta's inferior political position vis-à-vis that of Lagos. This resulted in the granting of an "independent" status for Abeokuta—the product of cooperation between the intelligentsia and the missionaries.[13] Further, the EUBM served as the springboard for Saro participation in local Abeokutan politics. This was to make all the difference in the world. Hence, it was the new elite, and not the traditionalists, who harped for faster change in Abeokuta.[14]

The EUBM ultimately failed because of a dispute with Governor Glover of Lagos and internecine dissension over the accession of Ademola I as the Alake of Abeokuta in 1869. This date marks the fission point in the grand coalition between the traditionalists and the modernists. It also marks the de facto demise of the EUBM. The board itself lived on in skeletal form through the tenacity of purpose of Johnson until 1874,[15] when Johnson, having quarreled with the authorities in Abeokuta, moved to Lagos.

The EUBM was an attempt to build a stable government from the top. Consequently, the board was out of touch with the people. Its failure marked, in part, the fact that the Egba remained attached to their traditional forms of government. The Saro could not forge what they considered to be a more viable political system, one in tune with the realities of urban living, cultural change, and proximity to an imperial administration from Europe.[16] The traditionalists among the Egba were not yet ready to relinquish authority to the Saro. The recognizable unit of government remained the township, derived from the old town in the Egba forest.[17] However, political inroads had been made by the new elite.

At this point, in order to accentuate the advances in Abeokuta toward modernity, let us briefly compare Abeokuta's government with that of a neighboring town. A comparable town was Ibadan, only twenty miles northeast of Abeokuta.[18] Here, because of conditions surrounding its inception, the town had not even begun to develop a governmental machinery resembling Abeokuta's in sophistication during the time of the EUBM. Ibadan developed in its early years as a war camp. Afonja, an ambitious kakanfo (generalissimo) of the Old Oyo Empire residing in Illorin, sought to make himself the Alafin (king) of the empire. For this purpose, in 1813, he invited the marauding Fulani to help him. Since the Fulani were on their own jihad (the establishment of the Fulani Empire of Usman dan Fodio), they seized upon the opportunity. They quickly overran the whole area, killing Afonja, and levying tributes on the towns that were not destroyed. From 1813 to 1840, several attempts were made by the Yoruba to throw off the Fulani yoke. They failed, due largely to internal rivalry and jealousy—the Yoruba civil wars. The Oyo deserted southward, taking part in the Owu war, already referred to, and founding the settlements of Modakeke and Ibadan—a deserted, but not destroyed, Egba village. Established as a war camp in 1830, Ibadan continued to be ruled by the military. Although most of its inhabitants were of Oyo extraction, the town was under the protection of Ife. This situation was bound to cause internal strife as the Oyo disliked being ruled by an Ife general. As it was continually engaged in warfare, a strong, but elemental, government was established in the new town under the nominal sovereignty of imperial Oyo and the administration of the Bale (king) of Ibadan.[19] The town was not really able to settle down to municipal development until 1893 when Governor Carter concluded a peace agreement between the opposing armies and established a British resident to aid and advise in the changeover to a peacetime administration. Although from this point on, Ibadan quickly developed its municipal superstructure, in the nineteenth century it offers an example of a town in the same vicinity as Abeokuta that was clearly at a different stage of political sophistication.

The Egba United Government, 1898-1914

Following the collapse of the EUBM, and without a forceful figure such as Johnson on the scene, the educated elite did not have a council to sit on and very little direct influence in Abeokuta for twenty-four years.[20]

The intelligentsia as a whole received new life only when Abeokuta gained independence in 1893. They sent missions to Lagos and Governor McCallum to try and iron out the strained relations that had developed between Lagos and Abeokuta over the expansionist motives of the Lagos government. A series of consultations followed. The tripartite participants in the negotiations were the traditional and westernized elites of Abeokuta, the Lagos Egba residents, and the colonial secretary. The result was that the governor traveled to Abeokuta in 1898 and assisted in the creation and establishment of the Egba United Government (EUG).[21]

The creation of the EUG was another success for the educated elite. The death of Alake Oyekan in 1881 ushered in the comparatively uneventful reigns of Alake Oluwajin (1881-1891) and Alake Osokalu (1891-1892). This period was followed by the accession of Alake Gbadebo I (1892-1920). He had gradually allowed real power to slip from his hands into that of the Olori Ologun (head of the war chiefs) and the traditionalists in the face of British designs against the independent status of Abeokuta. So the Saro, following their reemergence in 1893, formed an alliance with successful indigenous entrepreneurs and members of the Christian Missionary Society (CMS) against the traditionalists and the policies of Alake Gbadebo I. The alliance sought to make peace with British officials in Lagos and wrest control of government in Abeokuta from the Ologun. The result was the creation in 1898 of the EUG, which was a governing council with the Alake as chair.[22] The councilors were the Obas of the other three subsections in Abeokuta, an Ogboni representative, a senior Ologun, a senior Muslim chief, and a Christian chief. Although a majority of the council members were traditionalists, real power lay with a small administrative establishment that included a prosperous Egba trader, C. B. Moore, as its treasurer and an Amaro, P. O. Martins, as its secretary. Both were members of the new elite, equally established in Abeokuta and Lagos. The dominant personality in the new government, however, was that of J. H. Samuel, the EUG's executive secretary. Samuel was a clergyman and school principal who headed the prestigious Methodist Boys High School in Lagos. Upon moving from Lagos to Abeokuta, Samuel changed his name to Adegboyega Edun.[23] Once ensconced as the executive secretary of Abeokuta, Edun's officious demeanor rapidly deteriorated to being condescending toward Egbas while being accommodative toward British officials. This stance was probably necessitated by the fact that Edun depended so heavily on the military mediation of Lagos officials for the maintenance of his power.

A major achievement of the EUG was that it renewed the EUBM drive toward the modernization of governmental institutions in Abeokuta.[24] Another success was that it introduced political, administrative, and technical improvements to Abeokuta. These improvements advanced Abeokuta's local government services. In doing this, it aped the government of Lagos in many cases. For instance, the EUG created a colonial chaplain to the Alake, proliferated government departments, and created a huge bureaucracy. These same developments were, ironically, to contribute to the EUG's downfall. The top-heavy bureaucracy constituted a drain on the limited financial resources at its disposal. The EUG did not tax palm oil and cocoa, for most of its existence, because of Ogboni objections. A belated attempt to tax palm produce in 1912 had to be aborted because of the loss of independence and the fall of the government. Other contributory factors in the demise of the EUG were the split between Edun and other members of the intelligentsia and the failure of the new elite to continue carrying entrepreneurs and missionaries in partnership with them. The political mismanagement of the city disillusioned the new elite's allies. Furthermore, when it came to a show of force, the military in Abeokuta was not strong enough to maintain its independence from Britain. Perhaps the biggest single reason for the fall of the EUG was Edun's repeated reliance on soldiers from Lagos in Egba affairs. Governor Lugard in Lagos used the opportunity presented by the injection of Lagos troops to quell the local dissension known as the Ijemo rising to demand the surrender of Abeokuta's independence. He got it, backed up by superior firepower. Following British annexation of Abeokuta, the EUG council lost its role as a representative policy-debating organ and was demoted to being an appeal court with reduced membership.

The main difference between the EUBM and the EUG was that the EUBM received its backing and strength domestically from within Abeokuta. Conversely, the EUG was established in 1898 with external assistance from Lagos and sustained militarily, for instance in 1901 and 1903, by Lagos. The 1901 incident was over the Onitiri succession dispute. In 1903, the people of Kemta sought to usurp certain judicial rights of the Alake.[25] Both the EUBM and the EUG pursued an amalgamation of traditionalists and modernists, and both failed, partly because they could not sustain the coalitions that had established them. In 1914, the Egba National Council was instituted under Alake Gbadebo I. It lasted until 1920 when the newly crowned Alake Ademola II was made the sole native authority for Abeokuta.

The traditional elite were not interested in modernization. They were justifiably content with true and tested ways that had worked for them. Modernization was propagated by members of the Western-educated Saro minority. Their reasons included both a desire to contribute to the improvement of their homeland, since they were of Egba extraction, and a wish to provide employment opportunities, as well as political sway, for members of their class. The educated minority succeeded in obtaining support for modern measures from traditional leaders in periods when relations with the British were seen as threatening and when cooperation was important and potentially beneficial to the whole of Abeokuta. The new elite helped to fashion and advance Abeokuta's local government system.

The Alake of Abeokuta, Ademola II, 1920-1962.
Reproduced from the Nigerian *Daily Times*, May 25, 1939.

Alake Ademola II

We have seen how the intelligentsia played an important role in the nineteenth century local government structure of Abeokuta. Before recounting their contributions in the twentieth century, it will be necessary here to provide the background of the supererogative Alake, Ladapo Ademola, under whom Abeokuta clearly cemented its position as the model for native administration in western Nigeria.[26] It was the interaction between the Alake and the educated elite, together with the catalytic contributions of Egba women that provided the direction of Abeokuta's political development. This political sophistication gave Abeokuta its preeminent status among native administrations in Nigeria. The reasons for this position are the rapidity and quality of Abeokuta's changeover from a single ruler to a democratically appointed council as its local government unit. This constitutional amplification was of general application in western Nigeria, but Abeokuta exemplified it better than any other town. Hence, its "model" reputation!

Born in Abeokuta on September 20, 1872, Prince Ladapo Ademola was the first Yoruba Oba to receive any sort of lengthy political apprenticeship prior to succession to the throne. On the death of his father, Alake Ademola I, in 1877, Prince Ladapo was put in the care of his aunt Mrs. Oladunjaye Adefolu[27] to be raised in Lagos. His Lagos connections—particularly Balogun (formerly, an Ogboni title for an army general) Majekodunmi, a friend of his guardian, and Balogun Sogeinbo, an uncle—were to serve him in good stead and provide insight into Egba politics. After leaving school at the age of sixteen, Prince Ladapo served for two years as an apprentice printer. He then started the *Lagos Weekly Record* in 1890 as an assistant to John Payne Jackson, a prominent Lagos politician. While on the staff of the *Record*, Ladapo met such colorful personalities as G. W. Johnson, the leading light of the EUBM, and R. B. Blaize, the famed "wealthiest man in Lagos." Ladapo's gregarious nature and boundless energy enabled him to be successful in business. During this period, he watched the interests of Abeokuta and acquired the political and diplomatic experience and savvy that he would later demonstrate.

In 1897, Prince Ladapo made his first attempt at political involvement in Abeokutan affairs. In that year, he organized a meeting of Egba chiefs to receive Governor Henry McCallum.[28] This event led to better understanding and more cordial relations between the Egba government and the colonial authorities. By the early years of the twentieth century, Prince Ladapo had emerged as an unofficial ambassador of the Egba and aide to Alake Gbadebo I.

Prince Ladapo's first real inroad into Egba politics was his work during 1898 in persuading Governor McCallum to revive the title of Osile of Oke-Ona so that that section of Abeokuta would once again have its own Oba. Prince Ladapo then strove to unite the four sections and make them the basis of a unified government—the EUG.[29] In this way, Ladapo demonstrated an ability to work with the intelligentsia early in his political career. Ladapo very capably straddled the two elites in Abeokuta, in that he was a literate member of the royal family. Hence, his sympathies could go either way. In 1899, the prince was again instrumental in negotiations between Egba chiefs and the Lagos government for the construction of a railway pass into Yorubaland through Egba territory.[30] By elucidating the virtues of such a move to the Egba chiefs, the threatened use of force by the Lagos government on this issue became unnecessary. The chiefs were afraid that the railway would facilitate the emigration of Abeokuta's youth.[31] With the railway, however, came further progress and development.

Prince Ladapo Ademola's dexterity in handling difficult situations showed itself once more in the aftermath of the Adubi riots incident of 1918. This incident was the culmination of the abrogation of Abeokuta's independence and the introduction of direct taxation and forced unpaid labor in Abeokuta. Imperial troops were brought in and were still there when Prince Ladapo became Alake Ademola II in 1920 upon elevation to the Obaship of Egbaland. He immediately pressed for the removal of the troops, confident in the belief that they would never again be needed in Abeokuta as long as he was Oba.[32] They were not! The new Alake did not want the intervention of troops between himself and his people. His word that there would be no more riots and his prior good relations with the British administration were sufficient to secure the removal of the troops.[33] He was the first of the truly powerful Alakes of the modern era.

At the age of forty-eight, Alake Ademola II was initiated into office by Governor Hugh Clifford amidst scenes of enthusiasm and splendor unprecedented in Egbaland.[34] Oba Ademola II lived a spartan, frugal existence. He was an abstainer from both cigarettes and alcohol. He was a tireless worker. A typical day for him started at five in the morning and ended at night with short breaks in the morning for devotional exercises in his private chapel. As a Christian, he was in good standing with the new elite while his relationship with members of the traditional elite was not adversely affected. Respite took the form of evening relaxation for perhaps an hour in the summer garden spent in either peaceful meditation or easy study of his goldfish. He possessed a tireless and active mind, exhibited boundless energy, and was an impartial arbiter.[35] On the negative side, he was accused of being unable to make friends easily. This accusation rested on the colorable fact that many of his political supporters and kingmakers later became openly hostile to him. The Alake's response to this charge was that while he did not intend to make enemies, he resented sycophantic friends who attempted to unduly dominate his policies.[36] This was a bold stance! He was also accused of being domineering, relentless, and ruthless. Such is the high-profile liability of assuming the appurtenances of responsibility!

Alake Ademola II was a well-traveled man. Always an Anglophile, he visited England in 1904 as a member of the suite of Alake Gbadebo II, his predecessor. [37] He visited England again in 1936 on the occasion of the coronation of King George VI. He maintained correspondence with his English friends the Duke of Windsor and the Duke of Kent. Perhaps because of experiences garnered in his travels abroad, as well as his early preparation for office, he was described in 1939 as being "without doubt the ablest of the Yoruba rulers."[38]

Upon confirmation as the Alake, the British made Ademola II the sole native authority for Abeokuta. This was in keeping with their indirect-rule notion of identifying a prominent local chief and ruling through him.[39] The Alake, however, chose to rule with a council made up of sectional Obas and general chiefs. It was to be known as the Egba National Council (ENC). The ENC was the first attempt of Ademola II, as the Alake, to reorganize Abeokuta's political structure. The ENC was formally opened in 1926 by Major U. F. Ruxton, then lieutenant governor of the Southern Provinces.[40] The ENC existed from 1926 to 1939.

Let us briefly examine the structure of the ENC. Both the EUBM and the EUG had been attempts to rule from the top. Without reorganizing the village government structure, the intelligentsia wanted a new overall governing body for Abeokuta. The Alake wanted to reorganize from the grassroots up. His aim was "to fuse all the sections of Egbaland into one undivided people so as to present a united front."[41] To do this, he would create three sectional councils and seventy-two township councils as the basis of government. Ake section did not have a council of its own but was represented by the Alake. We have already noted how the Alake fought for the revival of an Oba for Oke-Ona in 1898 so that all sections would have an Oba. Everyone belonged to a township with its own council. Each township was part of a section, and the section sent representative Obas to the Alake. Since the sectional Obas had no authority other than in their own districts, it was important to have senior Ogboni chiefs who could coordinate their efforts by having executive powers in any quarter of Abeokuta. These were the ten general-titled chiefs. These chiefs were Ogboni because they had the traditional sanction of being kingmakers. Over the years, they gradually acquired the position of chief advisor to the Alake and constituted an inner council where all important matters were discussed before they were dealt with in council.

Accordingly, for the first time in Abeokuta's history, the introduction of the ENC ushered in a vertical, as well as a horizontal, plane to the town's political structure. Although an improvement over previous administrations, this new council had several flaws. For one thing, the ENC took no cognizance of the intelligentsia. Their place in the hierarchy had been effectively taken over by the Ogboni inner council. Most Ogboni were traditionalists; hence, there was a built-in source of discontent. By omitting the new elite from government, the Alake was perhaps overcompensating for those who had helped him into office and not fully recognizing the changing political atmosphere in Abeokuta. The township councils were also not truly representative of the people in those townships. They were closed societies for the traditional elite and, thereby, not sufficiently open to public opinion.[42] Furthermore, the township councils did not send representative nominees to the sectional councils. The ENC, therefore, was bound to fail; and it did!

The interaction between the Alake and the new elite created the dynamic of political action in Abeokuta from 1939 to 1952. This chapter has delineated the profile of those two political factors in Abeokuta. The contributions of the Saro to Abeokuta's political system were expressed through the EUBM and the EUG. These two governments were the first inclusion of the Saro in Egba politics. They served also to democratize Abeokuta's government. This was important because it set the stage for the new elite's further participation in government after 1939. This participation, after the beginning of the Second World War, had to contend with the dominant personality of the Alake. This chapter has also sketched a personality profile of Alake Ademola II. Furthermore, Alake Ademola II's contributions to Abeokuta's government prior to 1939 have been illustrated.

The previous chapters have been a general discussion of Abeokuta's local government before 1939. The following chapter will focus on the years from 1939 to 1952. We will discuss the inclusion of women in Abeokuta's government. These suffragettes were members of the new elite, so their struggle for enfranchisement was really a continuation of the new elite's participation in government. We will also examine the circumstances surrounding the Alake's abdication from the throne of Egbaland and his later return to Abeokuta. The Alake's exile was of pivotal importance during the period under study. We will also delineate the continued participation of the traditional elite. Their renewed significance in local politics was crucial at this time.

SUGGESTIONS FOR FURTHER READING

Coleman, James Smoot. *Nationalism & Development in Africa: Selected Essays*. New York: Labyrinth Books, 1994.

Duiker, William J. *Twentieth-Century World History*. Belmont, CA: West / Wadsworth, 1999.

Gailey, Harry A. *Lugard and the Abeokuta Uprising: The Demise of Egba Independence*. Bodmin, Cornwall: Frank Cass, 1982.

Zachernuk, Philip. *Colonial Subjects: An African Intelligensia and Atlantic Ideas*. Charlottesville and London: University Press of Virginia, 2000.

INTERNET RESOURCES

The following Internet sites contain written and visual materials that are germane to this chapter.

Adebisi, Ebenezer. 1999. *Nigeria: National Questions and Challenges for the Next Millennium*. Abeokuta [Nigeria]: Falak Publishers.
    <http://www.lib.ohio-state.edu>
    Retrieved July 18, 2002

Adebowale, Siyanbade. 2000. *Development of Ife (1930-1980)*. [Nigeria]: Litchfield Nigeria.
    <http://www.lib.ohio-state.edu>
    Retrieved July 18, 2002

Africa: From Underdevelopment to Annihilation: A Contending Theoretical Perspective. Enugu, Nigeria: Auto-Century Publishing Company. 1999.
    <htpp://www.lib.ohio-state.edu>
    Retrieved July 18, 2002

Amadi, I. E. S. *Institutions Supporting Technological Change in Nigeria: The Role of Industrial Development Centers*, chapter 19.
    <http://www.idrc.ca/books/focus/790/chp19.html>
    Retrieved July 18, 2002

Institutional and Gender Ideals in Nineteenth-Century Abeokuta. New Approaches and the Politics of Change.
    <http://www.makerere.ac.ug/womenstudies/congress2/updates_politics. html>
    Retrieved July 18, 2002

Reflections on the Political Economy of Nigeria. Abeokuta, Ogun State: Goad Educational Publishers. 1999.
    <http://www.lib.ohio-state.edu>
    Retrieved July 18, 2002

Political Map of Nigeria

Location of Abeokuta in Nigeria

The reference for many Internet photographs is the following:
http:\\www.wikipedia.com\wiki\Abeokuta

EGBA TERRITORY—1918

Based on Map Enclosure
to Lugard's Confidential
Despatch, 15 August 1918
in C.O. 583/68

Abeokuta as seen from Olumo Rock.

The "Rock of Abeokuta," as seen around 1892

Partial view of Olumo Rock

Kuto Road in Abeokuta

Abiola International Soccer Stadium, dedicated to presidential
aspirant Chief M. K. O. Abiola

Banner placed outside the Alake's palace, October 2009

Archway of the entrance to the Alake's palace

Panoramic view of the entrance to the Alake's palace

Landscape view of the entrance to the Alake's palace

Renovated Cathedral Church of St. Peter, Ake, Abeokuta

New Cathedral Church of St. Peter

Original Cathedral Church of St. Peter, Ake, Abeokuta, the
first church in Egbaland, in Ogun State, and in Nigeria

Sacred Heart Hospital, Itesi. The first hospital in Abeokuta

Abeokuta Grammar (High) School frontal entrance, Idi Aba, Abeokuta

Abeokuta Grammar (High) School entrance, Idi Aba, Abeokuta

Inside Abeokuta Grammar (High) School. Idi Aba, Abeokuta

Inside Lisabi Grammar (Junior High) School, Idi Aba,
Abeokuta

St. John's Anglican Church (under reconstruction) October 2009

Madam Tinubu's statue in Lagos, Nigeria

Olumo Rock depicting the 2006 renovations

Olumo Rock renovations, depicting the old staircase and the
modern elevator, October 2009

Panoramic view of the Olumo Rock Fountain, October 2009

Close-up view of the Olumo Rock Fountain, October 2009

The 2004 foundation stone of the Olumo Rock Tourist Complex, dedicated by His Excellency Otunba Gbenga Daniel, the Governor of Ogun State

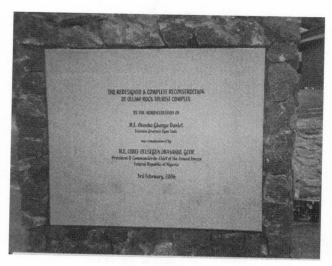

The 2006 foundation stone of the redesign and reconstruction of the Olumo Rock Tourist Complex, dedicated by His Excellency Otunba Gbenga Daniel, the Governor of Ogun State

View of the descent upon scaling Olumo Rock

L to R—Mrs. Kunbi Sodipo, Mrs. Bola Akisanmi, HRH Oba
Gbadebo III, regnant Alake of Abeokuta, Olori Tokunbo Gbadebo
(Alake's wife), Mrs. Soremi, and Mrs. Mustapha. Reception at
Majestic Restaurant, London, England. August 5, 2007

Alake Ademola II in the 1940s and 1950s—the central figure
during this period of study

Alake Gbadebo III, the regnant Alake of Abeokuta

CHAPTER 4

THE STRUCTURE AND PRACTICE OF NATIVE ADMINISTRATION IN ABEOKUTA

In this chapter, we will be concerned with two main topics: the Egba Central Council and the constitutional crisis that led to the abdication and later reinstallation of the Alake. We will examine the structure and practice of the Egba Central Council in some detail because it is an important governing body during this entire period. The Egba Central Council was inaugurated in Abeokuta along with the introduction of native administration. We will also look cursorily at the Egba war effort, the conferences of chiefs of the western provinces, and compare Abeokuta to two other areas of the western provinces in order to note the problems of those areas. Having described a fully functioning Egba Central Council, we will now be in a position to examine in detail the three stages leading to the abdication of the Alake: his resignation as the sole native authority for Abeokuta, his voluntary exile to Oshogbo, and his abdication in 1948. The circumstances surrounding his return to Abeokuta, and subsequent reinstallation as the Alake, will also be recorded. In 1952, the local government law ushered in a new phase in local government. We will note this and what it meant for Abeokuta.

The Egba Central Council (1939-52) Up to 1946

As the Egba National Council (ENC) did not prove to be a functional success, a new organization was clearly required. This new council came into being as a recommendation contained in the Abeokuta Intelligence Report. Governor Cameron required his political officers to produce intelligence reports for each of the provinces in Nigeria so that the British might better understand the customs and history of the people whom they ruled. In April 1939, based on these reports, the southern provinces of Nigeria were divided up into two groups of six provinces each, east and west with their capitals at Enugu and Ibadan respectively. Neither the Alake nor the educated elite was the author of the new constitution. Resident Miller, in writing the report, decided to regard this new council as a resuscitation of the Egba United Government rather than link it to the Alake's own first attempts at reorganization in 1926. He felt that the Egba National Council lacked historical longevity, although only twenty-eight years younger than the Egba United Government. It was to be a modern Egba United Government with extended membership.[1] He built on the Egba National Council, however. The new council was to be known as the Egba Central Council (ECC). It was to be an advisory council with no powers of legislation in itself. The ECC existed in Abeokuta from 1939 to 1952. Abeokuta was the first town in western Nigeria to have an advisory council under the native-administration system. The Alake was, however, still theoretically the sole native authority for Abeokuta.

Since the Egba Central Council was a very important body during the period under study, let us look further into how it was constituted. The ECC was made up of the Alake as president, general-titled chiefs,[2] the sectional Obas, and sectional council nominees in rotation. The inner council was abolished. The sectional council nominees came from reconstituted sectional and township councils. The township meetings were now to be open to everybody. Representatives went from township councils to sectional councils, and on to the Abeokuta city council. There were to be sixty-seven councilors, including both life and elected members, from the sections of Abeokuta.[3] The councilors were made up of twenty-nine representatives from the Egba Ake section, nine each from Gbagura and Oke-Ona and four from Owu, making a total of fifty-one councilors. To them were added fourteen ex officio members from the elite and the Obas from the two districts of Otta and Imale.[4] The heads of the Christian and Muslim religions were now to be elected from their townships.[5] It was also agreed

> that the council should include four educated gentlemen (members of the new elite) if possible one from each of the four sections. This sectional representation should not be made the rule and it should be left to [the Lagos] Government's discretion to select the four most suitable men.[6]

The new elite were to be represented

> because the Native Authorities of today have to deal with so many modern problems that they should have the benefit of the best education and intelligence that there is in the place.[7]

In this way the Alake, the sectional Obas, and the general-titled chiefs would have the benefit of the opinion, not only of the other chiefs as with the Egba National Council, but also of the new elite and the general public in Abeokuta. The opinions expressed by the people would receive consideration from that council best suited to deal with them.

It was proposed that the Egba Central Council should meet once a month and that all committees should be directly responsible to it. The sectional councils were to meet once a month before the central council meeting and were to have an opportunity to discuss the agenda to be presented to the ECC.[8] The sectional councils were also given various executive duties. Governor Bourdillon approved the reorganization proposals,[9] and the new Egba Central Council met for the first time on March 4, 1941.[10] The inaugural session was formally opened by C. C. Whitely, CMG, the chief commissioner of the western provinces.

Insofar as the revised Egba Central Council was planned on more democratic lines and included men of letters who ostensibly had progressive ideas, it was a definite advance over its predecessors—the Egba National Council, Egba United Government, and the Egba United Board of Management. It satisfied the criticism of the learned who complained that they were not welcome in local government because they were perceived as a threat to the natural leaders. It was no longer necessary for many of the new elite to seek jobs with the Lagos government.[11] The ECC organization was also fully representative of the elite. It further showed that British recommendations for the reorganization of a local government unit could meet with the approbation of a natural ruler and still satisfy the general public. The general populace in Abeokuta at this time was not politically active. Government was not abusive. As long as the common good was not undermined, power struggles at the top could go on unabated. Nor did it matter that either a Christian, Muslim, or animist leadership ruled. Nonetheless, many Egba were nominal Christians by this time.

The British-sponsored transition to a reconstituted Egba Central Council went smoothly in Abeokuta. This was in contrast to some other towns in Yorubaland. The Ekiti region of Yorubaland is an instance of an area where the proposed British reorganization of the Ekitiparapo (Ekiti United Government) was not welcomed by the Obas and people of the area. The official reason for the reorganization of the southern provinces was to try to create more geographically satisfactory and administratively convenient local government units. Reorganization did satisfy the aims of administrative officers, but in Ekitiland, they erred in their perception of the Ekitiparapo (the federation constituted in 1877 to combat the military menace of Ibadan). While accepting itself as part of the whole, each of the sixteen towns in the federation cherished its autonomy. This was not apparent to any British official observing the federation at work during the Kiriji war (1879-1886). The British sought to employ the federation as the basis for the working of the indirect-rule system in the Ekiti and Ijesha areas.[12] However, Ado-Ekiti, the major town in Ekiti, wished to form a separate native-authority district. Ado-Ekiti's desire for independence was rebuffed by British officials on the grounds of territorial inconvenience for administrative purposes. Ado-Ekiti was the geographical and commercial center of Ekiti, and its independence would have meant that the component parts of the federation would have been geographically separated.[13] However, the acting chief secretary, western provinces, did reluctantly advocate the granting of independence to Ado-Ekiti.

Another instance of dissatisfaction with the alignment into divisions was in Warri Province. The Abraka clan under Kwale native administration, being Urhobo, were not satisfied with their alignment with Igbos and wanted a transfer to the western Urhobo native administration.[14] The system of native administration had been introduced into the Kwale division on October 1, 1927.[15] In these early days, each village was regarded by the political officers as a separate unit or native court area, its relationship to other villages being a matter of minor importance as compared with territorial convenience from the officers' point of view.[16] The people of Abraka clan now wanted this anomaly corrected. While other examples of adverse reaction to reorganization in the western provinces proliferate in Benin, Ibadan, and Ilesha for example, Abeokuta did not experience these kinds of problems. This was so largely because it had an evolved administrative base from which to build. Reorganization had something to build on in Abeokuta because the ethnicity of the Egba was distinct, and the structure of their government was well defined. The refashioned Egba Central Council covered more than just administrative remodeling, however. Closely related to the problem of structure was the problem of finance.[17] Although on the whole the system of tax collection was fairly satisfactory, the machinery was improved and made more efficient. The sectional Obas, instead of residing in the districts for the purpose of supervising the collection of taxes, were encouraged to pay only occasional visits of one or two days' duration to the districts for the purpose of collection. The collection of the tax itself was to be a feature of responsibility for the village council.[18]

The new Egba Central Council also addressed itself to the question of education. While the responsibility for education lay largely with the central government in Lagos, the Egba local government took the lead in its perspicacious educational policy. Several schools were established in Abeokuta, including the Oba Ademola II School (established in 1945), the Abeokuta Girls' School, and the Owu African Church School. Generous grants were made by the local government from sparse funds for their upkeep.[19] Abeokuta probably had more schools than any other town in western Nigeria.

One major reorganization plan did not come to fruition, however. This pertained to the native court system. The significance of this system for our study is that Abeokuta was the only place in southern Nigeria where a court president was not a chief. Instead, a qualified barrister was president. This emphasized the role of the new elite in government. At this time, it was a Mr. Folarin who presided over the A court. It was recommended that appeal should lie directly from the A court to the high court in Lagos and that the Alake's court be abolished.[20] The Egba Central Council rejected this proposal. Courts of B, C, and D grades remained unchanged.

The provision of courts was next in importance to schools for most native administrations in western Nigeria. The reason for this was that, as Lord Hailey pointed out, the native courts were thought of as representing a purely native sphere in which the people could manage their own affairs.[21] The composition of these customary courts was usually made up of the elite.

The central ordinance establishing the native court system was Ordinance No. 44 of 1933. The courts had their powers spelled out in the warrants setting them up. The powers were to extend over "civil and criminal cases in which all the parties belonged to a class of persons who have ordinarily been subject to the jurisdiction of native tribunals."[22] The jurisdiction conferred on the courts was to be regulated in accordance with native law and custom.[23] Most of the cases they handled were connected with land and the question of ownership.

The various approved, and implemented, provisions of the Egba Central Council propelled Abeokuta into a position as the paragon of local government bodies in Nigeria under British colonial rule. These provisions also ensured that throughout the Second World War, order was maintained in the domain of Alake Ademola II.

The Abeokuta war effort owed a great deal to the encouragement and good work in government being performed by the Alake. Egba sons were encouraged to join the army. Abeokuta organized dances, the proceeds of which were sent to London. The Egba were able to buy a spitfire called Abeokuta for allied use. Egba farmers' rubber and palm kernels were vitally essential to the prosecution of the war.[24] Rubber was needed for tanks, guns, airplanes, and tires; kernel oil was needed for high explosives for the army and navy and bombs for the Royal Air Force. After the war, a Southeast Asia Contingent Troops Reception Committee was set up in Abeokuta to welcome home and rehabilitate the members of the troops of Egba extraction.[25] Perhaps in recognition of the war effort of the Egba, the Alake, already a Commander of the British Empire (CBE) was made a Companion of the Order of St. Michael and St. George (CMG) by King George VI of England.[26]

Another instance of the good work of the Alake was his part in establishing the Conference of the Chiefs of the Western Provinces. Modeled after the Conference of the Emirs of the Northern Provinces (inaugurated in 1925), this Western chiefs' conference came into being in March 1937.[27] The aims and objectives of the conference were to deepen affection, goodwill and confidence and to facilitate cooperation among the Obas and their chiefs and people and furthermore to obliterate all the tribal jealousies and rivalries of the past.[28]

The conference later served as the archetype for the Western House of Chiefs, the upper house under the local government system. The Alake hosted the conference in 1940.[29] It was at the Abeokuta meeting that the name of the conference was changed from the Conference of Yoruba Chiefs to the Conference of the Chiefs of the Western Provinces. The Alake felt that the time had come to invite Obas from the non-Yoruba districts of the western provinces, such as Warri Province, and to have them take part in the deliberations.

A sore point in many of these conferences was the perennial question of chieftaincy disputes.[30] This was a problem for all the native administrations of the west. The disputes arose over the question of rotation among the ruling houses eligible to present candidates for chieftaincy titles.[31] In many cases concerning the lesser chieftaincies, the princes had to be forced to accept the throne as they shrank from the arduous responsibilities of the office. By the beginning of the 1940s, this reluctance had changed to inordinate ambition. Members of the elite were now encouraged to break the rotation and seek stools because, unlike in the past, they had become paid positions. As presidents of courts of law, they received sitting fees. Many of the new elite, as lawyers, earned fees from chieftaincy disputes that went to court. Hence, they fanned the disputes, often entering them themselves to keep the flames of dissention alive.[32]

Many paramount chiefs complicated the disputes by aiding their sycophants to become junior chiefs under them. In addition, the indirect-rule system, by its need to identify chiefs, only served to elevate chieftaincies, sometimes beyond their traditional positions.[33] Under the British, if there was no clear-cut, traditionally sanctioned, dominant Oba for an area, such as in Ekiti, then one was created. This made it easier for the British to rule through him. Abeokuta had its share of these disputes. The Alake was placed in the untenable position of having to adjudicate in many of them. It was a predicament certain to make some political enemies. In the early 1940s, the Alake was entangled in disputes over the lesser chieftaincies of the Osi of the Egba,[34] Lisa of the Iporo,[35] and Abese of the Egba.[36]

The Period of "Progressive" Unions

In this section and the next, we will be concerned with the power struggles in Abeokuta that led to the abdication of the Alake. This was a three-part process. Firstly, the Alake decided by mid-July 1948 to relinquish his position as the sole native authority for Abeokuta. Secondly, by the end of that month he decided to go on self-exile. Thirdly, at the end of December, he was forced to abdicate. We will examine all three stages.

From 1946 to 1950, factional wrangling among the Egba created a constitutional crisis in Abeokuta that led to the abdication, and subsequent restoration, of the Alake. This crisis was precipitated by the demands of the leadership of Egba women that taxation for women in Abeokuta be abolished and, subsequently, that they be granted representation on the Egba Central Council. Later in the political crisis, the position of the women was strengthened by the help of a section of the Ogboni chiefs. They wanted the restoration of their ancient rights. This period saw the intersection of many political alignments for and against the Alake. It will be necessary to identify these groups. The factions can be termed progressive unions and may be divided generally into what Curtin has described as "neotraditionalists" and "defensive modernizers."[37] Both groups saw change as inevitable, but the neotraditionalists wanted, and were willing to pay the price for, greater modernization than were the defensive modernizers. No one group remained definable in any one category, however.

The two most important unions for the purpose of this study are the Abeokuta Women's Union (neotraditionalists), an association of market and professional women and part of the Nigerian Women's Union, and the Egbe Atunluse (gentrification society), a conservative organization of defensive modernizers for men and women dedicated to peace in Egbaland. The Abeokuta Women's Union was the renamed Abeokuta Ladies' Club, founded in 1923 by Mrs. Kuti and invigorated in March 1944 to include female entrepreneurs and represent their concerns.[38] Some unions were formed for *ad hoc* purposes. These would include the Egba Youth League. There were also unions formed outside Abeokuta but consisting of Egba in the diaspora who were interested in, and speculating upon, affairs at home. These would include the Egba Young Men's Society and the union based in Lagos for the drawing up of a new constitution for Egbaland in 1950. In June 1948, the Egbe Omo Oduduwa was inaugurated in Ife to cover the whole of Yorubaland.[39] The primary purpose of the Egbe Omo Oduduwa (society of the descendants of Oduduwa—the cultural hero and mythical progenitor of the Yoruba) was to

> enable the Yoruba to tackle objectively problems peculiar to them as an ethnic group in order to remove any potential obstacle in their way of marching towards their common objective[40] of "a virile, modernized and efficient Yoruba state with its own individuality within the Federal State of Nigeria."[41]

These unions existed alongside established unions such as the Ogboni Society and the Majeobaje Society (the society for the preservation of Egbaland, formed secretly in 1947), a conservative union for men and women. As their numbers increased, the new elite broke up into smaller groups. The progressive unions were formed because the broad, general objectives of the new elite had been acquired. Also, since the Alake was educated, he anticipated many of their general programs. Further, many of the new elite were becoming sufficiently absorbed into their society to want benefits in common with other classes of society. Hence many of the "progressive" unions cut across class and emphasized programs and professions instead.

In the political alignments for the soul of Egbaland, the Abeokuta Women's Union, Majeobaje Society (whose president at this time was Rev. I. O. Ransome-Kuti, Mrs. Kuti's husband), Egba Youth League, together with the chiefs from Ake section among the Ogboni, all opposed the Alake while only the Egbe Atunluse fought consistently for the Alake retaining his office. The Egbe Atunluse became important late in this period. The Egbe Omo Oduduwa and Lagos Egba intermittently tried to mediate in the constitutional crisis. We must remember that the new elite were no longer a political unit.

The Alake Goes into Voluntary Exile

The Abeokuta Women's Union was the first of the progressive unions to test its constitutional position in Abeokuta. On June 27, 1946, the Abeokuta Women's Union addressed a petition to the Egba Central Council on behalf of female Egba entrepreneurs. Although marginalized by the indirect-rule system and victimized by the Parakoyi, women in Abeokuta were important in the commercial sector where they decided "such things as market location, days, and prices of commodities and services."[42] The female entrepreneurs demanded better working conditions in the markets; free trade (restrictions having been imposed as a war exigency); a say in the management of their city-state, inasmuch as they paid taxes but were not "being represented in this council [the ECC] by [their] own representatives";[43] and the abolition of taxation for women as had been done in Ibadan. They felt that they were being doubly taxed: once in the marketplace and once through a poll tax. In the marketplace, the women were subjected to "conditional sales." "This was an attempt to force the burden of slower moving goods [such as cutlasses] onto the women traders. Since the vast majority of the market women survived on small margins of profit and had traditionally exercised control of the commodities' prices, conditional sales placed most of them in an even more precarious position."[44] The exercise of the poll tax, while being objectionable in principle, was also vexatious in its application because "homes were invaded and women were sometimes physically assaulted, including being stripped naked, ostensibly to assess their ages to determine their eligibility for taxation. And women were jailed for nonpayment of taxes."[45] Indeed, "women's taxation had been a sore point for many years in Abeokuta, where women were among the first females in Nigeria on whom the British imposed a tax. As early as 1917, a poll tax [or 'head'] tax was imposed on the people. This reflected London's philosophy that the colonies should bear the cost of their own 'development' and replaced the former systems of tribute payments and conscripted labor, which had included women."[46] As Johnson-Odim and Mba expressed it further,

> in fact, the issue of female taxation (and attendant to it, reform of the Sole Native Authority [SNA] system, including women's representation on it) would lead to the most dynamic and protracted of the women's struggles, culminating in both the temporary abdication of the Alake and reform of the SNA.[47]

The Abeokuta Women's Union proposed specific recommendations in lieu of their perceived injustices based on audits of the ECC. In the geographical expression that is Nigeria, taxation of women took place only in Abeokuta and Ijebu Provinces at this time.

The president of the Abeokuta Women's Union was Chief (Mrs.) Olufunmilayo Ransome-Kuti.[48] She is of signal importance as one of the premier suffragists in Nigeria. Mrs. Kuti was the first Nigerian woman to be

the death of Alake Ademola I in 1877, there was an acephalous period in Abeokuta before Oba Oyekan ascended to the throne in 1879 as the third Alake. The third interregnum was from 1881 to 1885—between the reigns of Alake Oyekan, the third Alake, and Alake Oluwaji, Abeokuta's fourth Alake. The fourth lapse in regal continuity lasted from 1889, after Alake Oluwaji's reign, to 1891, when Oba Sokalu became the fifth Alake of Abeokuta.

The interregnum meant that both Mrs. Kuti and the leadership of the women of Abeokuta, as well as the Ogboni, were able to flex their political muscles. The disenfranchised women received a boost in August 1948 by being represented on the Egba Central Council. The Ogboni regained a measure of their old powers under the guise of a democratic amendment to the unwritten constitution. They were showing the frustrations of being overshadowed by the new elite for so long. Further checks and balances could now be imposed into the constitution. Moreover, the Alake's exile demonstrated that a military coup was not necessary in Abeokuta to effect sweeping political changes.

The self-exile of the Alake and his demise as the sole native authority for Abeokuta was of signal importance for the native-administration system. It pointed to the position of Obas in Yorubaland after the Second World War.[76] The native-administration system was based on the retention of power by the monarchs. This position was challenged and undermined much more after the war than before it. The chiefs were not to be permitted to dominate their people.

> The root cause of most tensions between Yoruba communities
> and their paramount chiefs was the excess of power which had
> been vested in those chiefs by the British in disregard of customary
> limitations.[77]

The educated Anglophile elite throughout western Nigeria felt that the mantle of power fell on them. Yet it must be stressed that the new elite constituted a tiny minority, only 6 percent of Nigeria's population in the early 1950s. Although they hoped, by raising political consciousness to receive legitimacy for their right to govern by being democratically chosen, the generality of the populace regarded them with distrust and aloofness. Abeokuta was not an exception. The new elite were a small minority who sought, in a democratic manner, to be the arbiters of law, order, and justice. However, they were viewed with detachment by the people outside their ranks.

The Alake Returns to Abeokuta

After the self-exile of the Alake, the Egba Central Council became the native authority for Abeokuta. The Egba Central Council held its first meeting as native authority in a full house and an over spilling gallery on August 19, 1948.[78] The Oluwo of Ijeun, an Ogboni chief, was elected to the chair of the Egba Central Council. The president and vice president of the Abeokuta Women's Union became members of the Egba Central Council. In his speech declaring the house in session, Resident Blair said that for the first time, the Egba Central Council was the native authority for Egba Division and not merely an advisory council.[79] They had to be not just content with following the wishes of the people; they had to also lead them. They had to make decisions that would have the force of law under the Native Authority Ordinance. The two most pressing problems attacked first by the Egba Central Council were the questions of Abeokuta's financial situation[80] and law and order.

The period from mid-1948 to the end of 1950 was the nadir of Abeokuta's constitutional position vis-à-vis other towns in the western provinces. During this period, the Women's Union was in a continuing power struggle with the Egbe Atunluse as to which society would gain ascendancy in Egba politics. The Women's Union was against the return of the Alake while the Egbe Atunluse, the conservatives dedicated to peace in Abeokuta, was for it. The Egbe Atunluse became very prominent at this time. The significance of this era is that there was no strong personality in the political constellation. As such, government suffered. The Egba had always functioned better under a strong leader. This vacuum was filled by expatriate members of the regional authority who increasingly became a feature in the political factions of Abeokuta. Not since the early days of the reorganization of the southern provinces had British political officials intervened so directly in Egba affairs.

In January 1949, an extraordinary meeting of the Egba Central Council was held to consider a letter dated December 31, 1948, sent to the Egba people through the resident in which the Alake stated that conditions had not improved in Abeokuta and that those conditions had forced him to "unhesitatingly bow, therefore, to the inevitable by surrendering hereby the office of Alake of Abeokuta."[81] This was his formal letter of abdication. Erstwhile, he had simply been in self-exile, choosing to resign in stages. He expressed the desire to return to Abeokuta at any time there was a change of heart. Much to the dismay of the Egbe Atunluse, the council accepted his formal letter of resignation.

The Egbe Atunluse at this point decided to flex their political muscle. The Egba Central Council's unrepresentative nature now came under attack by the Egbe Atunluse. The Women's Union had opened the problem of representation in October 1948 when they tried retrogressively to promote the chair of the Egba Central Council as the sole native authority for Abeokuta.[82] A new Egba Central Council was chosen in June 1949.[83] The new body discussed the procedure for the selection of a new Alake in August 1949. During the same month, and at irregular intervals, Egba residing in Lagos sent delegations to Abeokuta to intercede. The Egba Central Council's attempts to reform the constitution were commended.

Political strife continued unabated in Abeokuta during 1950. In February of that year, a motion was moved in the Egba Central Council for the president and vice president of the Abeokuta Women's Union to be expelled from the executive committee of the Egba Central Council to which they had been appointed. It was felt that Mrs. Kuti was too high-handed and constituted a disruptive influence in Egba Central Council deliberations. This move was met with demonstrations by the women. However, in the same month, a splinter group arose against the united voice of Egba womanhood. The women's section of the Egbe Atunluse denounced the leadership of Mrs. Kuti. They accused her of "encouraging acts which were not conducive to peace and good administration in Egbaland."[84]

The wrangling of these political factions in Abeokuta preempted the energetic tackling of grave problems that had befallen the town. Famine was threatening as food was shipped out of town for better prices elsewhere.[85] Also, food production was down in the area owing to the unsettled state of affairs. There was, in addition, the problem of disease to be tackled. These problems pointed to the urgency of how badly the acephalous ship of state was floundering. Sometimes people had to be reminded of their own history. The lesson learned during the Alake's exile was that the Egba are best served by a strong central personality in government. Much as sections of the people might prefer to rule without the Alake, the passage of time showed that the smooth operation of government needed his vitality and experience. Clearly, Abeokuta lacked direction at this time. Something had to be done.

In July 1950, the question of the ex-Alake's return to Abeokuta was introduced in the Egba Central Council.[86] A final and decisive resolution allowing the Alake to return to Abeokuta was passed on November 30, 1950, by a vote of twenty-nine to nineteen with some abstentions.[87] This was over the very active objections of the Women's Union and the Majeobaje Society, the direct intervention of the regional authority, constitutional wrangling over rules and a quorum for the Egba Central Council, and a citywide referendum. The Egba Central Council decision was communicated to the Alake.

So after twenty-nine months of exile, twenty-four months of which were as a private citizen, the ex-king once more became Oba Alaiyeluwa Ademola II, CMG, the Alake of Egbaland. Ladapo Samuel Ademola returned to Abeokuta on December 3, 1950. The official statement of his return was made by the chief commissioner, western provinces. It read,

> On the 30th of November, 1950, the Egba Central Council, a majority, voted for the recall of Ademola to the traditional office of Alake of Abeokuta.
>
> After full consideration of the vote, and having regard to the wishes and interests of the Egba people, the Alake decided to resume his traditional office and returns to Abeokuta on the morning of December 3. His return was made with the knowledge and consent of Government.[88]

The Alake broadcasted to his people at 6:00 p.m. on December 3, 1950, from Abeokuta. In stating that he had returned according to the wishes of his people, he averred,

> I hereby solemnly and sincerely declare that I shall return as a constitutional Oba and that I shall cause no interference, either directly or indirectly, with the administration of the affairs of the Egba Native Authority beyond executing the normal duties required as chairman of the Egba Council.
>
> I hereby promise that I shall take no revenge of any nature against any person or persons who may have opposed my return in the past.[89]

Stating his future policy, the Alake concluded, "I hereby pledge myself to the furtherance of peace, progress, and prosperity among the Egba people, and I call upon all members of the public to unite and support me in this aim."[90] There were no incidents during the day of his return. The return of the Alake marked the re-establishment of stability to the town as the Alake made it his first priority to heal the political wounds of Abeokuta. The erstwhile warring factions now slowly began to close ranks behind him.[91] Opposition did not disappear, but many chiefs now openly came out in support of the Oba, confessing that it was a bad mistake to have forced him into exile.[92] After the rapprochement, the Alake began to work hard to regain the confidence and goodwill of his people. Being a modernist, he realized that only with this understanding could Abeokuta recapture its lost ground as the model for other political administrations in Nigeria—a position that it had temporarily surrendered.

The Local Government Law of 1952

Abeokuta in this era clearly demonstrated that the old order was giving way to the new. The period of dominance by traditional chiefs was ending. This phenomenon was taking place all over the western provinces. Election into councils was no longer by reason of advancement in years. Institutionalized police forces were replacing special collections of hunters and blacksmiths who gathered in times of emergency to protect their towns. Structured trades and industries and agricultural committees and departments were also replacing more or less individual trade efforts by the citizenry of towns. All these trappings required a new political vehicle.

That vehicle was to be known as local government as distinct from native administration. Beginning in the 1950s, names that are synonymous with "statesmanship" in Nigeria began to appear, first on the local governance scene and, later, on the national stage. Eminent Yoruba personalities such as Chief Obafemi Awolowo of Ikenne, Chief Samuel Akintola of Ogbomosho, and Chief T. A. Odutola of Ijebu Ode became distinguished political icons. Chief Awolowo and others (including the author's cousin, Chief Ohu Babatunde Akin-Olugbade, the Balogun of Owu and Ekerin Alake, fourth in line to the Alake[93]) organized the first Yoruba-based political party known as the Action Group (AG) in 1950-51.[94] Prominent Egba politicians now moved on to the regional and national scenes with the creation of the Western Region House of Assembly and the preparation for national independence.

The old rivalries surrounding the exile of the Alake found regional expression when the antagonistic organizations merged either with the Action Group

or the National Council of Nigeria and the Cameroons (NCNC).[95] These
affiliations were in common with general alignment into political parties
at this time. The Egbe Atunluse associated with the AG, which attracted
the new and rising class of the affluent and those in the highest levels of
professional and educational achievement.[96] Many chiefs and members of the
elite also joined the AG. The Abeokuta Women's Union and the Majeobaje
Society were aligned with the NCNC, which at this time was attracting
dissatisfied elements, particularly anti-tax advocates, farmers, traders, and
manual and clerical workers (mainly Igbos) in the urban areas of the western
region.[97] The Alake found political expression in the newly created Western
House of Chiefs, the upper house of the regional legislature. Together with
the Oni of Ife, Sir Adesoji Aderemi II, the Alake became a leader among
the paramount Obas of Yorubaland under the new order.

The resultant provincial legislation that culminated from all these allopatric
activities was the Western Region Local Government Law of 1952. The
passing of the law brought the system of native administration and indirect
rule to an end. This was a byproduct of the Macpherson Constitution
of 1951, which marked the final stage to full responsible government in
Nigeria. The transition from indirect rule to local government started in
1948 with the first African conference held in London[98] and the subsequent
landmark communiqué of the Creech Jones dispatch to Nigeria.[99] The
transition encompassed the discrediting of the Richards Constitution as
being inhibiting to southern Nigeria and being carried on without the full
consultation of the educated elite of the country. The period of conferences
in Nigeria ended with a systematic review of a new constitution from the
village level up to the regional level.

The local government law, which was really a part of the process that
resulted in the Macpherson Constitution, differentiated the new government
structure from the old. The factors that set local government apart from
the indirect-rule system were its democratic and popular elections; its direct
responsibility to the people and not to the central government in Lagos; a
high degree of popular participation; its range of functions, which were wider
than those of the native authorities; and its multilayered-tier structure. The
passing of the law virtually ended the local and parochial preoccupation of
the new elite with municipal government. The talents and energies of the
new elite of Abeokuta were now exercised on a regional basis for the most
part. The institutional changes that they had been responsible for would

not be undone, however. The process of democratization had changed the thinking of all concerned with local politics.

In this chapter, we have seen the culmination of the process of democratization begun in the nineteenth century by the new elite. In Abeokuta, the position of the new educated elite in government was secured permanently with the establishment of the Egba Central Council in 1939. The Egba Central Council structure took into account almost all shades of opinion in Abeokuta. The only group that did not receive direct representation was the women of Abeokuta. This was amended later. The structural problem having been settled, the Egba Central Council then concentrated on affecting such social services as education. From 1920 to 1962, Abeokuta had a stalwart Oba. The Alake's skills were demonstrated by his prominent role during the Conferences of the Chiefs of the Western Provinces, by his handling of the chieftaincy disputes of the early 1940s and, by his guidance of the Abeokuta war effort during the Second World War. After the war, Abeokuta faced a crisis in government. The constitutional crisis that led to the exile of the Alake was precipitated by the demands of Mrs. Kuti's Abeokuta Women's Union that taxation for women be abolished and, subsequently, that they be granted a voice on the Egba Central Council. Representation came in 1948. The position of the women was strengthened by the help of some Ogboni chiefs, the Majeobaje Society (Conservation Society), and the Egba Youth League. The Ogboni insisted on the abdication of the Alake. The Women's Union wanted greater democracy while the Ogboni wanted the retention of traditional methods of government. Both cooperated against the Alake for different reasons. The Alake resigned gracefully in 1948 after doing all that he constitutionally could to retain his office. The intervention of the Egba in the diaspora at Lagos and the Egbe Omo Oduduwa (the Society of Oduduwa's descendants) could not prevent the Alake's fall. Oduduwa is the progenitor of the Yoruba. The Alake returned to Abeokuta in 1950 with curtailed powers. Alake Ladapo Samuel Ademola II reigned for forty-two years as king of Abeokuta until his death on December 27, 1962. In 1952, the local government law of that year ushered in the nationalist period in Nigerian history. It signaled the gradual shift in emphasis of some of the new educated elite from parochial to national politics. The new elite had brought about permanent changes in Abeokuta's governmental institutions. These were their major contributions to municipal governance in Abeokuta.

SUGGESTIONS FOR FURTHER READING

Ayoade, J. A. A., Elone J. Nwabuzor, and Adesina Sambo, eds. *Women and Politics in Nigeria*. Lagos: Malthouse, 1992.

Awe, Bolanle, and Alice Schlegle, eds. "The Iyalode in the Traditional Yoruba Political System," *Sexual Stratification: A Cross-Cultural View*. New York: Columbia University Press, 1977.

Awe, Bolanle. *Nigerian Women in Historical Perspective*, ed. Lagos: Sankore/ Bookcraft, 1992.

Byfield, Judith A. *The Bluest Hands: A Social and Economic History of Women Dyers in Abeokuta (Nigeria), 1890-1940*. Portsmouth, New Hampshire: Heinemann, 2000.

Coles, Catherine, and Beverly Mack. *Hausa Women in the Twentieth Century*. Madison: University of Wisconsin, 1991.

Damachi, Godwin Ukandi. *Nigerian Modernization*. New York: The Third Press, 1972.

Johnson-Odim, Cheryl. "Towards a Conceptual Framework for the Study of African Women," *Red River Valley Historical Journal*, vol. 4, no. 1, 1979.

———. "Grassroots Organizing: Women in the Anti-Colonial Struggle in Southwestern Nigeria." *African Studies Review*, vol. 25, nos. 2/3, (June/ September 1982).

———. "Class and Gender: A Consideration of Yoruba Women during the Colonial Period," *Women and Class in Africa*. Claire Robertson and Iris Berger, eds., New York: Africana Publishing Company—Holms and Meier, 1986: 237-254.

———. "Common Themes, Different Contexts: Third World Women and Feminism," *Third World Women and the Politics of Feminism*, Chandra Mohanty, et al., eds. Bloomington: Indiana University Press, 1991.

————. "Lady Oyekan Abayomi: A Profile," in *Nigerian Women in Historical Perspectives*, Bolanle Awe, ed. Nigeria: Sankore Press, 1993.

————. "Mirror Images and Shared Standpoints: Black Women in Africa and in the African Diaspora," *Issue*, vol. 24, no. 2 (Fall 1996).

————. "Actions Louder than Words: The Historical Task of Defining Feminist Consciousness in Colonial West Africa," *Nation, Empire, Colony: Historicizing Gender and Race*. Ruth Roach Pierson and Nupur Chaudhuri, eds. Bloomington: Indiana University Press, 1998.

————, and Margaret Strobel, eds. *Restoring Women to History*. Bloomington: Indiana University Press, 1999.

Little, K. *African Women in Towns*. Cambridge: Cambridge University Press, 1973.

Mba, Nina. *Nigerian Women Mobilized: Women's Political Activity in Southern Nigeria, 1900-1945*. Berkeley: University of California Press, 1982.

Ogbomo, O.W. *When Men and Women Mattered: A History of Gender Relations among the Owan of Nigeria*. Rochester: University of Rochester Press, 1997.

Peil, Margaret. *Lagos: The City Is the People*. Boston: G. K. Hall, 1991.

Robertson, Claire and Iris Berger. *Women and Class in Africa*. Holmes and Meier, 1986.

Smock, David R. *Cultural and Political Aspects of Rural Transformation*. New York: Praeger, 1972.

Sweetman, David. *Women Leaders in African History*. London: Heinemann, 1984.

Women in Nigeria (WIN). *Women in Nigeria Today*. London: Zed, 1985.

INTERNET RESOURCES

The following Internet sites contain written and visual materials that are germane to this chapter.

African Women's Studies
> *JENDA: A Journal of Culture and African Women Studies*
> *<http://www.jendajournal.com>*
> Retrieved June 20, 2003

History of Nigeria
> *<http://www.countryreports.org/history/nigehist.htm>*
> Retrieved February 26, 2003

The Role of Women in Things Fall Apart
> *<http://www.scholars.nus.edu.sg/landow/post/nigeria/women.html>*
> Retrieved February 26, 2003

Women in Colonial Nigeria
> *<http://www.scholars.nus.edu.sg/landow/post/nigeria/colonwom.html>*
> Retrieved February 26, 2003

Women in Nigeria Today
> *<http://www.scholars.nus.edu.sg/landow/post/nigeria/contwomen.html>*
> Retrieved February 26, 2003

Women in Pre-colonial Nigeria
> *<http://www.scholars.nus.edu.sg/landow/post/nigeria/precolwon.html>*
> Retrieved February 26, 2003

the ENC (1926-1939). The structural deficiency of this government was that it was a throwback to the days before the emergence of the Saro. The new elite were not represented. For the most part, they were not a major force in government during this period.

In 1939, native administration was introduced into Nigeria. This was a more careful systemization of the indirect rule's notion of governing people through their own developed political institutions. For this, a new government was inaugurated, the ECC (1939-1952). The Alake, traditional elite, and new Western-educated elite all had representation in this government. Until 1948, the development of Abeokuta and its fortunes as the model of good and progressive government in Nigeria rested on the interaction between the new elite and the Alake. The elite of the Ogboni and lesser chiefs played a decisive part in government only sporadically in the 1940s and 1950s.

New forces began to clamor for representation in local government during the 1940s. The most vociferous among these forces was Egba womanhood. Until the 1940s, representation by the new elite had systematically excluded women. Now because of excessive taxation and adverse trading facilities, the women of Abeokuta, through their leadership, sought to enfranchise themselves. They were successful in 1948. The scale of power was tipped decisively on the side of the Women's Union, ironically enough, by the traditional elite. The Women's Union represented Egba market and professional women. This grand alliance came about because each had something to gain. The women would gain representation on the Egba Central Council, while the Ogboni would recover a measure of their eroding power and influence. To achieve this, they used the highly emotionally charged atmosphere then prevalent in Abeokuta to insist on the abdication of the Alake and, by so doing, replace him with one of their own. After trying constitutionally but unsuccessfully to ward off the efforts to replace him, the Alake decided to go on voluntary exile in mid-1948. At the end of the year, he tendered his letter of abdication. The Egba Central Council now became the local government authority for Abeokuta while the Alake took up residence in Oshogbo.

The Egba Central Council, as originally conceived, represented more than just a broadening of the personnel of government. It addressed itself to the problems of finance, education, agriculture, and the judiciary. All of these underwent a thorough revamping. The system of taxation was simplified. Education was better financed, and schools for girls were established. Agricultural techniques were improved, and the judiciary saw structural changes imposed. By the end of 1950, however, the lack of a strong personality in government meant that urgent matters of state such as increased food production and the eradication of diseases were being neglected. A drive was started by the Egbe Atunluse for the return of the Alake to Abeokuta. After a citywide referendum and the intervention of the regional authority, the Alake returned to his traditional office at the end of 1950, though with fewer powers than before. Between 1950 and 1952, the Alake devoted himself to the healing of the political wounds of Abeokuta and attending to the malaise of the city.

By 1952, the national push for internal self-government expressed itself locally by the passing of the local government act and the creation of a bicameral, wholly Nigerian regional government. The press of national and regional politics now enticed some of the new elite away from parochial politics.[2] Abeokuta had been made the model of good government by the active politics of the new elite. The lessons learned in Abeokuta served as thorough preparation for the intelligentsia's participation in national politics. Much more importantly for Egbaland, they and the Alake had helped to provide Abeokuta with such services as a good educational system, health facilities, roads, electricity, water, and agricultural improvements. These services and the institutional framework that made them possible were to be of lasting effect. The approach to local government had been irrevocably altered. Local government in Abeokuta had been opened up to all in the town.

What we have illustrated in this book is the process of political institutional change in Abeokuta. This change was brought about by the direct participation of the new elite in government. In tracing the evolution of political institutions in Abeokuta, we have of necessity had to talk about the classes involved in that change. However, our principal focus has been on the changes themselves and not on the sociology of the personnel of government. Before the advent of the Saro to Abeokuta, government had been a closed organization for members of the traditional elite. By 1952, after many governmental formats, an irrevocable structure had been established for administrative units. Government was now open to all in Abeokuta.

Royle, Trevor. *Winds of Change: The End of Empire in Africa*. North Pomfret, VT: Trafalgar Square, 1998.

Soyinka, Wole. *The Swamp Dwellers, 1959*.

————. *The Lion and the Jewel,* 1959 and 1996.

————. *The Trials of Brother Jero, 1960*.

————. *The Interpreters, 1965*.

————. *The Road, 1965*.

————. *A Dance of the Forest, 1966*.

————. *Kongi's Harvest, 1967*.

————. *Madmen and Specialists, 1970*.

————. *Season of Anomy, 1973*.

————. *Collected Plays (including A Dance of the Forest, The Swamp Dwellers, The Strong Breed, The Road, The Bacchae of Euripides) 1973*.

————. *Collected Plays 2, 1975*.

————. *Myth, Literature and the African World*, 1976.

————. *Language as Boundary*, 1978.

————. *Ake: The Years of Childhood, 1981*.

————. *A Shuttle in the Crypt*, 1987.

————. *Idanre and Other Poems*, 1987.

————. *The Man Died*, 1988.

———. *Art, Dialogue & Outrage: Essays on Literature and Culture*, 1988.

———. *Isara, a Voyage Around "Essays."*, 1991.

———. *The Open Sore of a Continent: A Personal Narrative of the Nigerian Crisis.*, 1997.

———. *The Trials of Brother Jero and the Strong Breed*, 1998.

———. *The Burden of Memory, the Muse of Forgiveness*, 1998.

———. *Soyinka*, 1999.

———. *Early Poems*, 1999.

———. *Conversations with Wole Soyinka*, editor: Biodun Jeyifo. 2001.

———. *Death and the King's Horsemen.* 2002.

———. *Samarkand and Other Markets I Have Known, 2002.*

———. *"You Must Set Forth at Dawn: A Memoir."* 2006.

Stremlau, John J. *The International Politics of the Nigerian Civil War, 1967-1970.* Princeton: Princeton University Press, 1977.

Thomas, Caroline and Peter Wilkins, eds. *Globalization, Human Security, and the African Experience.* Boulder, CO: Lynne Rienner Publishers, 1999.

Wright, Stephen. *Nigeria: Struggle for Stability and Status.* Boulder, CO: Westview, 1998.

INTERNET RESOURCES

The following Internet sites contain written and visual materials that are germane to this chapter.

Biography of Akinwande Oluwole Soyinka
    <http://www.scholars.nus.edu.sg/post/soyinka/soyinkatl.html.> n.a.

Clarke, Simon, Owen, Trefor, and Palmer, Susan L. 1999. *Local Government Elections in Nigeria: December 5, 1998.* The Report of the AAEA/IFES Joint International Observers Mission (Association of African Election Authorities and International Foundation for Election Systems). *<http://www.ifes.org/afrassoc1/afrassoc/nigeriafinalrep.htm>* Retrieved January 1, 1999.

Esajere, Akpo. 2003. *The patriots ask for interim government.* *<http://lwl4fd.law14.hotmail.msn.com/cgi-bin/getmsg?curmbox=F0000000 01&a=d38f5d5d214e2662658033c9>* Retrieved May 24, 2003. Personal Communication.

Fast facts about Nigeria: *Africa 2003* *<http://www.allafrica.com/img/commerce/africa 2003/nigeria.pdf>* Retrieved March 12, 2003

Global Literacy Project—Global Citizens—Classroom. "Nigeria—History since 1960" *<http://www.glpinc.org/Classroom%20Activities/ Nigeria%20Articles/Nigeria-history%20si . . . >* Retrieved February 26, 2003

History of Nigeria *<http://www.countryreports.org/history/nigehist.htm>* Retrieved February 26, 2003

Library of Congress Country Studies. "Nigeria: Emergence of Nigerian Nationalism" *<http://lcweb2.loc.gov/cgi-bin/query/r?frd/cstdy:@field(DOCID+ng0032>* Retrieved February 26, 2003

Library of Congress Country Studies. "Nigeria: Further Development of Colonial Policy" *<http://lcweb2.loc.gov/cgi-bin/query/r?frd/cstdy:@field (DOCID+ng0031>*
Retrieved February 26, 2003

Library of Congress Country Studies. "Nigeria: Politics in the Crisis Years" *<http:// lcweb2.loc.gov/cgi-bin/query/r?frd/cstdy:@field (DOCID+ng0034>*
Retrieved February 26, 2003

Library of Congress Country Studies. "Nigeria: Unification of Nigeria" *<http://lcweb2.loc.gov/cgi-bin/query/r?frd/cstdy:@field(DOCID+ng0030>*
Retrieved February 26, 2003

Nigerian Literature: Oral and Written Traditions *<http://www.scholars.nus.edu.sg/landow/post/nigeria/orality.html>*
Retrieved February 26, 2003

The Embassy of Nigeria: The May 5, 1999, Constitution of the Federal Republic of Nigeria *<http://www.nigeriaembassy.nl/gov.htm>*
Retrieved February 22, 2003

The Nigerian Congress—online: Overview of Administrative Levels. <http://www.nigeriacongress.org/fgn/administrative/lgs.asp>
Retrieved February 22, 2003

The Local Government Areas of Nigeria: Ogun State *<http://www.nigeriacongress.org/fgn/administrative/lgabystate.asp?state= Ogun>*
Retrieved February 22, 2003

Today's news about Nigeria *<http://www.gamji.com>*
Retrieved July 7, 2003

<http://www.gamji.com>
Retrieved Dec. 5 2009

Photography of Akinwande Oluwole Soyinka *<http://www.Nigeria-Arts.net/Literature/Novel/Wole_Soyinka/>* n.a.

END NOTES

1. Richard Goff, et al. *The Twentieth Century: A Brief Global History.* 5th ed. Boston, MA: McGraw-Hill, pp. 48, 221, 1998.

2. Vaughn Findley Carter and John Alexander Murray Rothney. *Twentieth-Century World,* pp.177-180, 5th ed. Boston, MA: Houghton Mifflin Company, 2002.

GLOSSARY

abdication. To relinquish power or responsibility formally

Abeokuta. A town in western Nigeria and the current capital of Ogun State

abrogation. To abolish; do away with; annul

acephalous. Headless, or lacking a clearly defined head; having no leader

admix. To mix, blend

aegis. Protection; sponsorship; patronage

Agura. The king of the Gbagura section of Abeokuta

Alafin. The king of Oyo

Alaiyeluwa. His Royal Majesty

Alake. The king of Abeokuta and the paramount monarch of Egbaland

allometric. The study of the change in proportion of various parts of an organism as a consequence of growth

allopatric.   Occurring in separate, non overlapping geographic areas, especially at the same time

aloofness.   Unfriendliness; detachment

amalgamation.   Merger; incorporation

Amaro.   Emancipated repatriates from Brazil

anachronism.   The representation of something as existing or occurring at other than its proper historical time

annex.   Take possession of; seize; take over; capture

anomalous.   Uncharacteristic; out of the ordinary

anomie.   Social instability; social alienation

appellation.   Designation; title

ardent.   Passionate; enthusiastic

arduous.   Difficult; demanding

Are-Ona-Kakanfo.   The title of Are-Ona-Kakanfo recalls the military days of the Yoruba when that title personified the feared commander in chief of the army whose position it was to continually enlarge the Yoruba Empire

asseverate.   To declare seriously or positively; affirm

autochthonous.   Descended from the inhabitants of the region in which it is found

aver.   To affirm positively; declare

avuncular.   Of or having to do with an uncle; similar to an uncle

babalawo.   A priest of the Ifa Oracle

Badagry.   A town in western Nigeria

Balogun.   Traditionally, a Balogun was a preeminent war chief. The title has retained its high profile and elevated status into contemporary times. As a kingmaker, a Balogun must now maintain the customs and traditions of the people whom he represents while simultaneously espousing their anomie as well as their prosperity.

bellicose.   Belligerent; aggressive; warlike; confrontational

Benin.   A town in Midwestern Nigeria and the current capital of Edo State

bucolic.   Rural

bulwark.   Protection; fortification; safeguard

burgeoning.   Growing; escalating

cadre.   A small group of trained personnel around which a larger organization can be built and trained

cession.   A ceding or surrender of territory; something given up

chieftaincy.   The office of the leader or titular head of a people or similar ethnic group

circumjacent.   Surrounding; lying around

CMS.   The Church Missionary Society; the first Anglican organization to establish in Abeokuta in 1846

cognate. Allied; related

comity. Considerate behavior toward others

condescension. Disdain; superciliousness

consanguineously. Relationship by blood, whether lineal (for example, by direct descent) or collateral (by virtue of a common ancestor); the degree of relationship by blood

consular. The affairs of an official appointed by a government to reside in a foreign country and represent that government's commercial interests and assist its citizens there

cowrie (or cowry). Seashells that were used as currency in the South Pacific and Africa

cursorily. Superficially; hastily

Dahomey. West African country, now renamed Benin

delineate. Define; outline; describe

deputation. Delegation; group of representatives

dissension. Opposition; disagreement; dissent

ebullition. A sudden outbreak of violent emotion

educated elite. Manumitted slaves who returned to Nigeria in the 1830s and 1840s. Those who returned directly from Sierra Leone became known as the Saro while those who returned from Brazil were known as the Amaro.

Egba.   An ethnicity among the Yoruba

Ekerin of Egbaland. An Ekerin of Egbaland, the fourth in line to the throne, is a member of the Alake's cabinet, representing the people of Owu. The Ekerin of Egbaland might serve as a member of the Alake's suite or, upon request, personate him at any ceremony or function.

émigrés.   People living abroad permanently

epexegesis.   Additional explanation or explanatory material

eradication.   Abolition; annihilation

erstwhile.   Former; previous

eschew.   Avoid; shun

ethnography.   The branch of anthropology that deals with the scientific description of specific human cultures

evangelize.   Convert to one's own religion; be an advocate for a cause

evince.   To show or demonstrate clearly; manifest

ex officio.   Benefit resulting from one's official position

federation.   Amalgamation; alliance; coalition

fictive.   Imaginative; inventive; fictional

Gbagura.   The third section of Abeokuta to establish in the metropolis

gerontocratic.   Government by elders; governing elders

gregarious.   Outgoing; sociable; extroversive

harbinger.   Forerunner; herald

hegemony.   Supremacy; domination

hermeneutic.   Interpretive; exclamatory

hinterland.   Vicinity; adjacent to a coastal area; surrounding area

homophyly.   Resemblance arising from common ancestry

Ibadan.   A town in western Nigeria and the current capital
                        of Oyo State

Ifa Oracle.   The religion of the Yoruba with Olorun as the
                        Supreme Being

Ife.   A town in western Nigeria

Ijaye.   A town in western Nigeria

Ijebu.   An ethnicity among the Yoruba

Ilugun.   A town in western Nigeria

immix.   To commingle; blend

inception.   The beginning of something, such as an understanding;
                        a commencement

incongruous.   Made up of disparate, inconsistent, or discordant
                        parts or qualities

interrogate.   To examine by questioning formally or officially

internecine.   Of or related to a struggle within a nation, organization, or group

interregnum.   The interval between the end of a sovereign's reign and the accession of a successor

irenicism.   Tending to promote peace and reconciliation

irrevocable.   Impossible to retract or revoke

Iporo.   A town in western Nigeria

Iwarefa.   The highest grade of six Ogboni chiefs (later known as the Alake's inner chiefs)

Iyalode.   The head of the women of a designated group among the Yoruba

laconic.   In brief; concise

Lagos.   The economic and social center, and the erstwhile capital, of Nigeria

linchpin.   A central cohesive element

manumit.   To free from slavery or bondage; emancipate

maraud.   To rove and raid in search of plunder

miscegenation.   Interbreeding of different races or of persons of different racial backgrounds

neolocal.   (Of a married couple) living together at a new residence

neophyte.   A beginner or novice

nexus.   A means of connection; a link or tie

numinous.   Spiritual

Oba.   A Yoruba king

odu.   An unwritten, sacred assemblage of religious, as well as social, and philosophical Yoruba knowledge

Oduduwa.   The progenitor of the Yoruba

Ogboni.   The most powerful traditional association in Abeokuta; a secret society; councilors

Oke-Ona.   The second section of Abeokuta to establish in the metropolis

oligarchy.   A form of government in which supreme power is vested in a few people

Olodumare.   God as creator of the universe. This is the preferred spelling by traditionalists

Ologun.   Yoruba war chiefs. They were in charge of the formation of the army

Olorun.   The Yoruba Supreme Being, the creator of the universe. This is the spelling that is preferred by modernists who believe in one God.

Olori.   The title of the wife of an Alake

Olori Ologun.   Head of the Yoruba war chiefs

Olumo Rock.   The central geographical feature of Abeokuta under which the original inhabitants found shelter in 1830 from marauding solders

omnibus.   Collection; compilation

omnipotent.   All-powerful; invincible

Oni.   The king of Ife

ontology.   The branch of metaphysics that deals with the nature of being

orisas.   Yoruba gods and goddesses

Osile.   The king of the Oke-Ona section of Abeokuta

ostensibly.   Apparently; presumably

Oyo.   A town in western Nigeria

Parakoyi.   They supervised trade and formed the local chamber of commerce

paramount.   Supreme; chief

parochial.   Provincial; unsophisticated

paternalistic.   Doing things for someone that the person ought to do independently, thus debilitating the individual.

perennial.   Occurring annually; returning

personate.   Represent

perspicacious.   Having or showing penetrating mental discernment; clear-sighted

posit.   Self-assertion; to propound an idea

precursor.   Forerunner; ancestor; predecessor

progenitor.   Ancestor; predecessor

proselytize.   Evangelize; convert

propitiation.   The means of warding off justifiable anger; offering a sacrifice in order to avert evil

protectorate.   Territory; colony; ruled province

punitive.   Disciplinary; corrective

quasi.   As though; almost but not quite; false

repatriate.   Send home; send back

resuscitate.   Revive; breathe new life into; bring around; save; give artificial respiration to

salubrious.   Healthful; conducive or favorable to health or well-being

Saro.   Manumitted repatriates from Sierra Leone

Seriki.   Traditionally, a Yoruba army position

servile.   Too willing to agree with someone or to do anything, no matter how demeaning it may be

strife.   Trouble; conflict; discord; contention fighting; friction

suffragette.   A woman campaigning for women's right to vote during elections, especially one who participated in militant protests during the early twentieth century in the United Kingdom

suffragist.   A supporter of the extension of the voting right to a certain group, especially to women, or to all people beyond a particular age

supererogative.   Performed or observed beyond the required or expected degree

superlative.   Excellent; unmatched; best; outstanding; exceptional; unbeatable

transmogrify.   Change form grotesquely; to change the appearance or form of something, especially in a grotesque or bizarre way

truncate.   To shorten by, or as if by, cutting off

truculent.   Hostile; bad tempered; defiant; quarrelsome; aggressive; confrontational

unabated.   Still as forceful or intense as previously

unduly.   Excessively; overly; disproportionately; out of all proportion; unjustifiably; undeservedly

variegated.   Multicolored; spotted; dappled; flecked; varied

veneration.   Worship; adoration; reverence; respect; admiration

veritable.   Absolute; real; genuine; authentic; true; actual

vertiginousness.   Whirling or spinning on an axis; tending to change
                         frequently or suddenly

vie.   Compete; contest; contend

vociferous.   Vocal; loud; express one's opinion forcefully

Yoruba.   Description of both the people and language of the
                         predominant ethnic group in western Nigeria

Yorubaland.   The territory in western Nigeria inhabited
                         predominantly by the Yoruba

BIOGRAPHICAL ENTRIES

The following brief biographies of important personalities mentioned in this book represent an attempt to foster greater clarity and understanding.

Oba Adele I.   He was the king of Lagos who established initial formal trade relationships with Abeokuta in the 1830s.

Samuel Ajayi Crowther.   He was the first Anglican Bishop of West Africa.

Oba Akitoye.   He was the eleventh Oba of Lagos from 1841 to 1845. King Akitoye I was deposed as the Oba of Lagos in 1845 by his ambitious nephew, Oba Kosoko (1846-1851). Oba Akitoye I proceeded into exile in Abeokuta, his maternal home, before relocating to Badagry for greater safety. In 1851, he was reinstalled as the king of Lagos (1851-1853) in return for the stoppage of the slave trade. King Akitoye I died in 1853 and was succeeded by his son, Oba Dosumu (1853-1885), who lost a great deal of his traditional power when the British ceded Lagos in 1860.

Governor Glover.   Sir John Harvey Glover was the governor of Lagos from 1865 to 1872. Glover Hall in Lagos was built in his honor.

Oba Kosoko.

In 1846, Oba Kosoko deposed his uncle as the king of Lagos and was the Oba of Lagos at British inception into Nigeria in 1849. He was the nephew of Oba Akitoye.

Lord Lugard.

Frederick D. Lugard formulated the notion of indirect rule in Nigeria. This was an adaptation of the policy first articulated in India. By 1914, the British saw the formal establishment of colonial rule in Nigeria as that of transforming Nigerian traditional political systems rather than introducing English governmental structures.

Lord Palmerston.

He was the British secretary of state for foreign affairs who served in the Whig government of Lord Grey from 1830 to 1832. From 1832 to 1852, Lord Palmerston served both Whig (Lord Melbourne, Lord John Russell) and Tory (Sir Robert Peel) governments. He believed that the main objective of the government's foreign policy should be to increase Britain's power in the world. In 1855, at the age of seventy, Lord Palmerston became prime minister for his first stint until 1858. His second period of service as the prime minister lasted from 1859 to 1865. Lord Palmerston died on October 18, 1865, at the age of eighty.

CHRONOLOGICAL HIGHLIGHTS OF EGBA HISTORY

2,000-1,000 B. C.   Arrival of the antecedent Yoruba in Nigeria.

1774   Independence of the Egba from the tributary relationship with the Oyo Empire.

May 1, 1807   Abolition of the slave trade by England.

1830   Foundation of Abeokuta.

1830s-1840s   Arrival of the Saro and Amaro in Abeokuta.

1838   Initial return of manumitted transatlantic slaves.

1843   Visit of Rev. Townsend to Abeokuta.

1844   Sodeke became the first chief of Abeokuta until 1845.

1845   Somoye became the regent of Abeokuta until 1868.

1845   Establishment of the present site of Ake township.

1846   Establishment of the Christian Missionary Society in Abeokuta.

1848   Publication of first Yoruba primer.

1848   Egba Chiefs wrote to Queen Victoria of England.

1849   Arrival of the British in Nigeria at Lagos.

1849   Queen Victoria's letter of response read to Egba Chiefs.

1849   First corn mill worked in Abeokuta.

1851   First Dahomeyan invasion defeated.

1854   Okukenu became the first Alake of Abeokuta until 1862.

1854   Election of Oba Pawu as the first Olowu of Owu in Abeokuta.

1857   Expulsion of Madam Tinubu from Lagos.

1859   Publication of *Iwe Irohin*, the first newspaper in Nigeria.

1861   Arrival of the British in Abeokuta.

1862   Publication of the Holy Bible in Yoruba.

1863   First brick molded in Abeokuta.

1869   Ademola I became the second Alake of Abeokuta until 1877.

1879   Oyekan became the third Alake of Abeokuta until 1881.

1885   Oluwaji became the fourth Alake of Abeokuta until 1889.

1887	Death of Madam Tinubu.
1891	Sokalu became the fifth Alake of Abeokuta until 1898.
1893-1914	Independence of Abeokuta from Britain.
1898	Gbadebo I became the sixth Alake of Abeokuta until 1920.
1898	Telegraph station opened in Lafenwa.
1899	Death of Oba Karunwi, the Osile of Oke-Ona.
1901	Introduction of vaccination.
1902	Appointment of Adegboyega Edun as the Secretary of the Egba United Government.
1903	Sokori bridge opened by the Egba United Government.
1904	Alake Gbadebo I visited England and was received by King Edward VII.
1908	Foundation of Abeokuta Grammar School.
1909	Establishment of a corn crushing machine at Sapon.
1910	Oba Abolade enthroned as the Agura of Gbagura.
1911	Lanfewa bridge opened.
1914	Creation of the geographical expression of Nigeria.
1920	Sir Ladapo Samuel Ademola II became the seventh Alake of Abeokuta until 1962.

1963   Gbadebo II became the eighth Alake of Abeokuta
                      until 1972.

1972   Michael Mofolorunso Oyebade Lipede became the
                      ninth Alake of Abeokuta.

2005   Micheal Mofolorunso Oyebade Lipede, the Alake
                      of Abeokuta, died on February 3, 2005.

2005   Oba Michael Adedotun Aremu Gbadebo III
                      became the tenth and regnant Alake of Abeokuta
                      on August 3, 2005.

2009   Dr. Bolu Akin-Olugbade, Esq., became the
                      Are-Ona-Kakanfo on October 8, 2009.

Abeokuta itself was the first town in Nigeria that could boast of a printing
press, a newspaper—*Iwe irohin Yoruba* (Yoruba newsletter), electricity, tap
water, and Western education.

_____

Ajisafe, Ajayi Kolawole. *History of Abeokuta*. Lagus: Kash & Klare Bookshop,
1948. (First published in 1918).

<http://abeokuta.freeservers.com/History.HTM>
        Retrieved September 18, 2009

SUMMARY LIST OF EGBA FIRSTS IN NIGERIA

The following is a short list of firsts that all Egba can justifiably be proud of.

Chief M. K. O. Abiola: First elected president of Nigeria to be denied office and be later vindicated

Chief Simeon O. Adebo: First Nigerian permanent representative to the United Nations

Justice Adetokunbo Ademola: First indigenous head of any Nigerian judiciary

First African appointed to the bench of the Inner Temple, London

First Nigerian chief justice of the Federation

Bishop Ajayi Crowther: First African Anglican bishop of West Africa

Justice Taslim Elias: First Nigerian judge and president of the International Court at The Hague.

First Nigerian to obtain a Ph.D. in law

Professor Adeoye Lambo: First African deputy director general of the World Health Organization

Dr. Joseph Lambo: First head of the Herbal Practitioners of Nigeria

Justice Sigismund O.   First chief judge of the Federal High Court
Lambo:

Sir Herbert Macaulay: First political party leader in Nigeria

J. Olutunji Majekodunmi: First Nigerian medalist in international sports (1950 Commonwealth Games) and pioneer Nigerian Olympian (London 1948 and Helsinki 1952 Games)

Mrs. Kofoworola Moore: First West African woman graduate (Oxford University) and daughter of Eric Moore

General Olusegun   The head of state of Nigeria from 1975 to
Obasanjo: 1979.

First consecutively elected President of Nigeria—from 1999 to 2007.

Only Nigerian military head of state to voluntarily relinquish power to democratically elected civilian authorities, which he did in 1979

First Distinguished Fellow of the University of Ibadan

Chief (Mrs.) Toyin   First chartered accountant in Nigeria
Olakunrin:

Professor Gabriel O.   First Nigerian to obtain a Ph.D. from a
Olusanya: Canadian university

Lady Olufunmilayo   First woman in Nigeria to own and drive an
Ransome-Kuti: automobile

Sir Josiah Akinbomi Savage:	First Nigerian general manager of the New Nigerian Development Corporation (Ankpa Division), honored for having recovered coal in Ankpa, thus precipitating the dawn of the infrastructural age in Nigeria
Hon. Justice William Akibo Savage:	First judge to be honored by a valedictorian session of the High Court of Lagos State, Nigeria
Chief Adebola Sodipo:	First African manager at G. B. Olivant megastore, Lagos. Pioneer student, St. Gregory's College, Lagos, Nigeria
Dr. Joseph Deinde Sodipo:	First African acupuncturist
Professor Wole Soyinka:	First African Nobel Prize winner in Literature

Kuti, Hon. Justice Ademola. *Salute to Kabiyesi Alayeluwa Oba Dr. Adedapo Adewale Tejuoso,* p. 89.

Odunoye, Oladipo et. al., *Oba Oyebade Lipede: A Great Egba Monarch,* pp. 61-62.

Savage, Pamela Evelyn. *The Life and Times of Honorable Justice William Akibo Savage,* pp. 22-23.

BIOGRAPHICAL SKETCHES OF EGBA ELITE

The following brief biographies represent sketches of eminent Egba, both historical and extant. Any omissions are strictly ones of submission and not of commission.

===

Chief Moshood Kashimawo Olawale Abiola

(August 24, 1937-July 7, 2001)

Chartered Accountant

Disputed Winner of the 1993 Nigerian Presidential Elections

Chief M. K. O. Abiola was born in Abeokuta, Ogun State, Nigeria, on August 24, 1937. He attended Baptist Boys High School, Abeokuta, from 1951 to 1956. In 1961, he preceded to the University of Glasgow, Scotland, United Kingdom, from where he graduated in 1963 as an accountant.

Upon returning to Nigeria, he became the deputy chief accountant for the Lagos University Teaching Hospital from1965 to 1967. He then went on to hold many other positions, including being the controller for Pfizer from 1968 to 1969; the comptroller for International Telephone and Telegraph (ITT) from 1969 to 1970; vice president for ITT Africa and the Middle East, as well as chairman and chief executive, ITT Nigeria from 1971 to 1988. He became the founder and chairman of Concord Press of Nigeria in 1978. He was also an executive with Radio Communications; an associate of the Chartered Institute of Secretaries; a member of the Institute of Management; a member of the National Party of Nigeria (NPN) from 1979 to 1982, as well as the chairman of the NPN, Ogun State branch from 1979 to 1982; and appointed chairman of the presidential organizing committee for the NPN in 1989.

As a Muslim, M. K. O. availed himself of the custom of marrying severally. He, therefore, married Simbiat Atinuke Shoaga in 1960, Kudirat Olayinka Adeyemi in 1973, Adebisi Olawunmi Oshin in 1974, and Dr. Doyinsola Abiola Aboaba in 1981. He was blessed with six daughters and four sons. Amongst his traditional titles were those of the Baba Adini of Yorubaland, B'obajiro of Egbaland, Are-Ona-Kakanfo of Oyo, Bashorun of Ibadan, and Bada of Gbagura Moslems, Abeokuta.

Chief Abiola was the winner of the 1993 Nigerian presidential elections before he was disenfranchised, had the election results unjustly overturned, arrested, and imprisoned in June 1994 by Major General Sani Abacha. He collapsed suddenly on July 7, 2001, and died in prison.

Uwechue, Ralph. ed. *Africa Who's Who*. London: Africa Books Limited, 1991

===

Chief Simeon Olaosebikan Adebo

(October 5, 1913-September 30, 1994)

First Permanent Nigerian Representative to the United Nations

Born on October 5, 1913, Chief Simeon Olaosebikan Adebo was a seasoned administrator, diplomat, and lawyer. He was called to the Bar in 1948 and worked as a senior civil servant. He became the head of the civil service and chief secretary to the government of the western region in 1961. In 1962, he became Nigeria's first permanent representative to the United Nations. In 1968, he was appointed as the United Nations undersecretary general and executive director of the United Nations Institute for Training and Research. He resigned from the United Nations and returned to Nigeria in 1970. He held various appointments as chairman of commissions subsequent to his return to Nigeria. His last formal appointment was with the National Institute of Policy and Strategic Studies in Lagos. Chief Adebo died on September 30, 1994.

———

Adebo, Chief Simeon O. *Our Unforgettable Years.* Lagos: Macmillan Nigeria Publishers, 1984.

<http://people.africadatabase.org/en/person/17590.html>
     Retrieved April 19, 2006

===

Alhaji Dauda Soroye Adegbenro

(1909-1966)

Prominent Nigerian Businessman and Politician

Born in Abeokuta in 1909, Alhaji Dauda Soroye Adegbenro was a prominent Nigerian businessman. He was educated at Baptist Boys High School, Abeokuta, from 1923 to 1925 and at Abeokuta Grammar School from 1925 to 1927. Alhaji Adebgenro began his career by working for the Nigerian Railway (north) from 1930 to 1937, United Africa Company from 1937 to 1940, and then returned to the Nigerian Railway (Lagos) from 1943 to 1945. After his civil service career, he established and conducted his own businesses in commerce and farming until 1951. Alhaji Adegbenro's successful business career enabled him to pursue a political career. Theretofore, his first political involvement had been to represent Egba West in the Western House of Assembly in 1951. Subsequently, he held various ministerial appointments in the government of the former western Nigeria from 1952 until 1962, including the parliamentary secretary to the minister of local government, minister of lands and housing, and minister of local government. He was the leader of the opposition in the Western House of Assembly from January 1963 until October 1965. Up until 1971, he was also the western state commissioner for finance. He performed a holy pilgrimage to Mecca and Medina in 1957 and thus became entitled to use the cognomen "Alhaji" as a prefix to his name. Upon his return from Mecca, he submitted a report to government that led to the establishment of the Western Nigeria Pilgrims Welfare Board in 1959, with the principal duty of catering for the welfare of hajj pilgrims. Alhaji Adegbenro was installed as the Asiwaju of Owu in 1959 and the Balogun of Owu in 1961.

In May 1962, Alhaji Adegbenro became embroiled in perhaps his greatest political brouhaha. At this time, there was a growing rift within the Action Group between its leader, Chief Obafemi Awolowo, and his deputy and premier of the western region, Chief Samuel Ladoke Akintola. This contentious political development in western Nigeria came to a head when Alhaji Adegbenro, as an Awolowo supporter, was appointed premier of the western region by Governor Sir Adesoji Aderemi, the Oni of Ife. General anomie reigned in the western region following fast upon the heels of disorder in the House of Assembly as the new premier presented his credentials and requested that the government provide him with a vote of confidence. Following ebullition, both among the parliamentarians in the assembly and among their supporters outside, the region was placed under a state of emergency. The government was suspended, and Dr. Moses A. Majekodunmi was appointed as the sole administrator of the Western Region.

Alhaji Adebgenro was married and is survived by several children. His hobbies were farming and gardening.

_____

Who's Who in Nigeria, 1971.

Oba Isaac Akinyele, 1880 to 1965, Christ Apostolic Church (Aladura) Nigeria, 2002.

<www.dacb.org/stories/nigeria/akinyele_issac.html>
    Retrieved September 11, 2009.

==

Emmanuel Adebisi Adegbite

(November 1931—)

Barrister at Law

Emmanuel Adegbite was born in November 1931. He was educated at Offa Grammar School; at the College of Commerce in Liverpool, England; and at Ahmadu Bello University, where he studied law. He practiced law from 1968 to 1970 before he was appointed a magistrate. He is married with children. He is also a member of the YMCA and the Good Samaritan Society.

_____

Who's Who in Nigeria, 1971.

===

Sir Adetokunbo Adegboyega Ademola

(September 1, 1906-January 29, 1993)

First Indigenous Chief Justice of the Federation of Nigeria

Sir Adetokunbo Adegboyega Ademola was born on September 1, 1906, in Ake Palace, Abeokuta. His father was Alake Ademola II of Abeokuta. He graduated from Saint Gregory's Grammar School and King's College, both in Lagos. He then proceeded to England, where he earned his Bachelor of Arts (1928) and Master of Arts (1931) degrees from Selwyn College, Cambridge University. In 1934, he was called to the Bar (Middle Temple) in London. Upon returning to Nigeria, Sir Ademola was the first African to be appointed to the bench of the Inner Temple as a crown counsel in the Attorney General's Office (Nigeria) from 1934 to 1935. From 1935 to 1936, Sir Ademola worked as an assistant secretary at the Southern Secretariat in Enugu, in present-day Anambra State. He then decided to enter private practice from 1936 to 1939. In 1948, he served as a member of the Commission for the Revision of Court Legislation and was appointed as a magistrate of the Protectorate Court in 1949. In 1953, he became the third Nigerian to be appointed a puisne judge; and in 1955, he was appointed Chief Justice for western Nigeria, and thus became the first indigenous head of a Nigerian judiciary. In January 1957, he was honored as a Knight of the British Empire (KBE). Other honors were also bestowed upon him: in 1963 he was admitted as a Commander of the Federation of Nigeria (CFR); also in 1963, he was further venerated when he was appointed one of Queen Elizabeth of England's privy councilors; and in 1972 he was awarded a Grand Commander of the Order of Nigeria (GCON). In 1958, he became the first Nigerian Chief Justice of the Federation of Nigeria and remained in that position until 1975.

As an undergraduate, Adetokunbo Ademola found time to indulge in his avocations of playing cricket and soccer. Upon his return to Nigeria in 1934, he systematically translated his love of sports into establishing veritable and viable national sports facilities and perspectives while also promoting sports on a continental level within Africa. In 1958, he was elected as the president of the Nigerian Olympic and Commonwealth Games Association. In 1963, on the advice of Lord Exeter, a British member of the International Olympic Committee, Sir Ademola was invited to become a member of the International Olympic Committee with commensurate increased prominence for African sports. Membership on the International Olympic Committee also encompassed serving on the Commission of Enquiry for South Africa from 1966 to 1968. Furthermore, as a member of the Joint Commission II of the International Olympic Committee, he was active in fostering closer relationships between the International Olympic Committee and National Olympic Committees, especially those in Africa. In 1969, he was rewarded for his administrative puissance by being elevated to the executive board of the joint commission. He served in that capacity until 1973. His greatest disappointment in sports was that he was unable to convince his peers to stage either the Olympic or the Commonwealth Games in Africa.

Quite predictably, Sir Ademola presided over numerous landmark cases during his tenure on the bench. One of them was the momentous case of *Rex v. Esther Johnson* in 1953. Judge Ademola found Esther Johnson guilty of having murdered her lover, a European railway official, and sentenced her to death. This decision railed a storm of protest on then judge Ademola. Many Nigerians felt that Esther Johnson should not hang for her crime, and ultimately, Judge Ademola demonstrated his equanimity by commuting her sentence. Sir Ademola was adamant about two legal principles: the rule of law and the independence of the judiciary. These principles were amply illustrated by one case in particular. Sir Ademola's decisions on the Supreme Court are contained in the Nigeria Law Reports. However, Sir Ademola's judgment in the precedence-setting case of *E. O. Lakanmi and Another v. the Attorney General of Western State* (SC 58/59) may be celebrated as what Chief Folarin Coker, his eulogist, has termed "his finest hour." Succinctly, the case involved whether a legislative edict by the federal military government of Nigeria had the probative value of a judicial decision in curtailing appellant proceedings before a court of appeal. Lakanmi had an appeal pending before the Western State Court of Appeal when the proceedings were effectively aborted by the promulgation of three decrees of the federal military government. These decrees validated the orders of an administrative tribunal, which were the subject of the appeal. Lakanmi's attorney, therefore, decided to appeal to the Federal Supreme Court. In a convoluted decision, Sir Ademola, as the president of the Supreme Court of Nigeria, held that Decree No. 45 of 1968 was inadmissible because Lakanmi's daughter was not a public official. Furthermore, Sir Ademola held that Decree No. 45 of 1968 truncated the appeal before the Western State Court of Appeal. Sir Ademola also opined that the decree amounted to "nothing short of legislative judgment and an exercise of judicial power." Moreover, Sir Ademola's brief stated that the decree was ultra vires and, therefore, invalid; and it allowed the appeal. The brief was upheld by the other members of the Supreme Court of Nigeria, namely Hon. Mr. Justice G. B. A. Coker, Hon. Sir Ian Lewis, Hon. Mr. Justice Charles O. Madarikan, and Hon. Mr. Justice Udo Udoma. While opinions remain divided about the case, Decree No. 28 of 1970 ratified it, thereby validating its equanimity. The case may be regarded as an eloquent illustration of the independence of the Nigerian judiciary while endowing its purveyors with the mantle of being sensately stalwart jurists.

Sir Adetokunbo Ademola was a member of several professional, international, and philanthropic organizations. Some of these include being founder and chairman of the Lagos Metropolitan Club, a founding member of the Island Club in Lagos, vice patron of the Yoruba Club, also in Lagos, and chairman of the Nigeria Cheshire Homes. Sir Ademola's versatile social interests were amply demonstrated by his having served as the president of parochial organizations, such as the Reformed Ogboni Fraternity, as well as universal institutions, such as the Nigerian Red Cross Association. Quite naturally, Sir Adetokunbo Ademola was active in numerous judicial organizations, mostly with international predilections. Substantially, he was an executive member of World Peace through Law and vice president of the World Association of Jurists. He was also a member of the International Commission of Jurists in 1961, the International Olympic Committee in 1963, the Nigerian Institute of International Affairs, and the United Nations International Public Service Advisory Board. He was appointed as the chancellor of the University of Nigeria, Nsukka, Enugu State, in 1975. Additionally, he was also the first Lagos member of the United Nations Committee of Experts Advising on Labor Conventions and Regulations. Sir

Adetokunbo Ademola's first wife was Dorcas Molola Johnson with whom he had one son, Adenekan Adekunle Ademola. In 1939, he married his second wife, Lady Kofoworola Aina Moore, the first West African woman graduate and daughter of Eric Moore. Lady Kofoworola Moore earned her bachelor's from Oxford University, Oxford, England.

———

<http://www.thisdayonline.com/archive/2003/02/18/20030218law09.html>
   Retrieved August 13, 2003.

<http://www.uq.net.au/~zzhsoszy/states/nigeria/abeokuta.html>
   Retrieved August 13, 2003.

===

Alaiyeluwa, Alake Ladapo Samuel Ademola II

(September 20, 1872-December 27, 1962)

The Seventh Alake of Abeokuta

Eschew anomie! From 1920 to 1952, that was the political drive that energized King Ademola II, the seventh Alake of Abeokuta. Oba Ademola II succeeded not only in avoiding the breakdown of social and political structures in Abeokuta but also actually in improving Abeokuta's political fortunes. By so doing, in 1939, Alake Ademola II earned the approbation of being "without doubt the ablest of the Yoruba rulers" of western Nigeria. Oba Ladapo Samuel Ademola was the supererogative Alake under whom Abeokuta clearly cemented its position as the model for native administrations in western Nigeria.

Born in Ake Palace, Abeokuta, on September 20, 1872, Oba Ladapo Samuel Ademola was the first Yoruba Oba to receive any sort of lengthy political apprenticeship prior to succession to the throne. Prince Ladapo was raised in Lagos by his aunt, Mrs. Oladunjaye Adefolu, following the death of his father, Alake Ademola I, in 1877. His Lagos connections—particularly those of Balogun Majekodunmi, a friend of his guardian, and Balogun Sogeinbo, an uncle—were to serve him in good stead and provide insight into Egba politics. After leaving school at the age of sixteen, Prince Ladapo served for two years as an apprentice printer. He then started the *Lagos Weekly Record* in 1890 as an assistant to John Payne Jackson, a prominent Lagos politician. While on the staff of the *Lagos Weekly Record*, Ladapo met such colorful personalities as G. W. Johnson, the leading light of the Egba United Board of Management, 1865-1874, and R. B. Blaize, the famed "wealthiest man in Lagos." Prince Ladapo's gregarious nature, and boundless energy, enabled him to be successful in business. During this period, he watched the interests of Abeokuta from afar and acquired the political and diplomatic experience and savvy that he would later demonstrate.

In 1897, Prince Ladapo made his first attempt at political involvement in Abeokuta affairs. In that year, he organized a meeting of Egba chiefs to receive Governor Henry McCallum. This event led to better understanding and more cordial relations between the Egba government and the British colonial authorities. By the early years of the twentieth century, Prince Ladapo had emerged as an unofficial ambassador of the Egba and aide to Alake Gbadebo I.

Prince Ladapo's first real inroad into Egba politics was his work during 1898 in persuading Governor McCallum in Lagos to revive the title of Osile of

Oke-Ona so that that section of Abeokuta would once again have its own Oba, then uniting the four sections of Abeokuta and making them the basis of a united administration—the Egba United Government, 1898-1914. In this way, at an early stage of his political career, Prince Ladapo demonstrated an ability to work with the educated elite. Prince Ladapo very capably straddled the two elites in Abeokuta, in that he was a literate member of the royal family. Hence, his sympathies could go either way. In 1899, the prince was again instrumental in the negotiations between Egba chiefs and the Lagos government, for the construction of a railway pass into Yorubaland through Egba territory. By elucidating the virtues of such a move to the Egba chiefs, the threatened use of force by the Lagos government on this issue became unnecessary. The chiefs were afraid that the railway would facilitate the emigration of Abeokuta's youth. With the railway, however, came further progress and development.

Prince Ladapo's dexterity in handling difficult situations showed itself once more in the aftermath of the Adubi riots of 1918. This incident was the culmination of the abrogation of Abeokuta's independence in 1918 and the introduction of direct taxation and forced unpaid labor in Abeokuta. Imperial troops were brought in and were still there when Prince Ladapo became Alake Ademola II in 1920 upon elevation to the Obaship of Egbaland. He immediately pressed for the removal of the troops, confident in the belief that they would never again be needed in Abeokuta as long as he was Alake. They were not. The new Alake did not want the intervention of troops between himself and his people. His word that there would be no more riots, and his prior good relations with the British administration, were sufficient to secure the removal of the troops.

At the age of forty-eight, Alake Ademola II was initiated into office by Governor Hugh Clifford amidst scenes of enthusiasm and splendor unprecedented in Egbaland. Upon confirmation as the Alake, the British made Ademola II the sole native authority for Abeokuta. He was the first of the truly powerful Alakes of the modern era.

Alake Ademola II was a well-traveled man. Always an admirer of Great Britain, he visited England in 1904 as a member of the suite of Alake Gbadebo I, his predecessor. He visited England again in 1936 on the occasion of the coronation of King George VI. He maintained correspondence with his English friends the Duke of Windsor and the Duke of Kent.

The Abeokuta effort during the Second World War owed a great deal to the encouragement and good work in government being performed by the Alake. The Egba were able to buy a spitfire called Abeokuta for allied use. Egba farmers' rubber and palm kernels were vitally essential to the prosecution of the war. Rubber was needed for tanks, guns, airplanes, and tires; kernel oil was needed for high explosives for the British army and navy and bombs for the Royal Air Force. After the war, a Southeast Asia Contingent Troops Reception Committee was set up in Abeokuta to welcome home and rehabilitate Egba troops. Perhaps in recognition of the war effort of the Egba, the Alake already a Commander of British Empire (CBE) was made a Companion of the Order of St. Michael and St. George (CMG) by King George VI of England.

Another instance of the good work of the Alake was his part in establishing the Conference of the Chiefs of the Western Provinces. Modeled after the Conference of the Emirs of the Northern Provinces, which was inaugurated in 1925, the Western Chiefs' Conference came into being in March 1937.

The conference later served as the archetype for the Western House of Chiefs, the upper house under the local government system. The Alake hosted the conference in 1940. It was at the Abeokuta meeting that the name of the conference was changed from the Conference of Yoruba Chiefs to the Conference of the Chiefs of the Western Provinces. The Alake felt that the time had come to invite Obas from the non-Yoruba districts of the western provinces, such as Warri Province, and to have them take part in the deliberations.

From 1946 to 1950, factional wrangling among the Egba created a constitutional crisis in Abeokuta that led to the abdication, and later return, of the Alake. This crisis was precipitated by the demand of the leadership of Egba women that taxation for women in Abeokuta be abolished and, subsequently, that they be granted a voice on the Egba Central Council. Later, the women's position was strengthened by the help of a section of the Ogboni chiefs who wanted the restoration of their ancient rights.

In the political alignments for the soul of Abeokuta, Chief Olufunmilayo Ransome-Kuti's Women's Union, the Reverend I. O. Ransome-Kuti's Majeobaje Society, and the Egba Youth League, together with the chiefs from Ake section among the Ogboni, all opposed the Alake while only the Egbe Atunluse fought consistently for the Alake to retain his office. The interaction between the Alake and the new educated elite created the dynamic of political action in Abeokuta from 1939 to 1952. On July 29, 1948, however, Alake Ademola II decided to go on voluntary exile so as to avoid the bloodshed that those in opposition to him threatened. In a message to the resident, Alake Ademola bemoaned his fate. Conditions had arisen that obliterated from his people's memory his previous selfless services for and on their behalf. After fifty years of service to the city-state, twenty-eight of which were in the capacity of the sole native authority for Egbaland, he could not understand why so fierce an opposition should arise so late in his reign.

Thus, in the 118th year of its existence as a town, Abeokuta laid a precedent for itself. For the first time in their history, the Egba were faced with a case of abdication. The man who was largely responsible for the formation of the Egba United Government (1898-1914), the delicate handling of the years immediately preceding and following the loss of independence (1914-1939), and the smooth running of a British-revised Egba Central Council with only minor intermittent trouble (from 1939 up to 1948) was rejected by significant sections of his people. The Alake decided to serve his exile by taking up residence in Oshogbo.

In July 1950, the question of the ex-Alake's return to Abeokuta was introduced in the Egba Central Council (1939-1952). A final and decisive resolution allowing the Alake to return to Abeokuta was passed on November 30, 1950, by a vote of twenty-nine to nineteen with some abstentions. So after twenty-nine months in exile and twenty-four months as a private citizen, the ex-Alake once more became Oba Alaiyeluwa Ademola II, CMG. He returned to Abeokuta on December 3, 1950.

At 6:00 p. m. on the evening of his arrival back in Abeokuta, the Alake broadcasted to his people. He stated that he returned according to the wishes of his people. He went on,

> I hereby solemnly and sincerely declare that I shall return as a constitutional Oba and that I shall cause no interference, either directly or indirectly, with the administration of the affairs of the Egba Native Authority beyond executing the normal duties required as chairman of the Egba Council.

I hereby promise that I shall take no revenge of any nature
against any person or persons who may have opposed my return
in the past.

The return of the Alake marked the re-establishment of stability in the
town as the Alake made it his first priority to heal the political wounds of
Abeokuta. The erstwhile warring factions now slowly began to close ranks
behind him. After the rapprochement, the Alake began to work hard to regain
the confidence and goodwill of his people. Being a modernist, he realized
that only with this understanding could Abeokuta regain its efflorescence—a
position which it had temporarily surrendered.

Alake Ademola II lived a spartan, frugal existence. He abstained from
ingesting both cigarettes and alcohol. He was also a tireless worker. A typical
day for him started at five in the morning and ended at night with short
breaks in the morning for devotional exercises in his private chapel. As a
Christian, he was in good standing with the new elite while his relationship
with members of the traditional elite was not adversely affected. Respite
took the form of evening relaxation for perhaps an hour in the summer
garden, spent in either peaceful meditation or easy study of his goldfish.
He possessed a tireless and active mind, exhibited boundless energy, and
was an impartial arbiter.

On the negative side, he was accused of being unable to make friends
easily. This accusation rested on the colorable fact that many of his political
supporters and kingmakers later became openly hostile to him. The Alake's
response to this charge was that while he did not intend to make enemies,
he resented sycophantic friends who attempted to unduly dominate his
policies. This was a bold stance. He was also accused of being domineering,
relentless, and ruthless. Such was the high-profile liability of assuming the
appurtenances of responsibility! Prince Ladapo Ademola married Tegumade
Assumpcao Alakiya. They had one son, Sir Adetokunbo Adegboyega
Ademola, who became the first indigenous chief justice of Nigeria. Alake
Ladapo Samuel Ademola II died on December 27, 1962.

The Nigerian *Daily Times, May 25,* 1939- February 7, 1951.

===

Chief Gladys Ibijoke Iyabode Akin-Olugbade

(June 12, 1924-October 21, 1988)

Otun Iyalode of Ago-Owu

Chief Gladys Ibijoke Iyabode Akin-Olugbade is from the Abati-George family of Ago Ododo, Oke-Ona, Abeokuta. Her father, Adeboye Abati-George, was a pioneer Nigerian executive of NITEL, then known as Cables & Wireless Nigeria, and a deacon of the First Baptist Church, Lagos. Chief Iyabode Akin-Olugbade was born in Lagos on June 12, 1924, and attended Saint Peter's Primary School, Ajele, Lagos, from 1925 to 1931. She transferred to Baptist Academy, Lagos, then coeducational, for her secondary education. Her contemporaries at Baptist Academy were the Nigerian celebrities Justice Olumide Omololu, Mrs. Aba Johnson, and Chief Olu Akinfosile.

Parenthetically, Chief Akinfosile's protégé, Dr. Peter Olafioye, the prominent Nigerian poet, was provided an F1 immigration visa to enter the USA as a student by Occidental College, a prestigious liberal arts university in Los Angeles, before he transferred to the University of San Diego. Chief Akinfosile was the Nigerian minister of communications at that time. Once ensconced in San Diego, Dr. Olafioye then encouraged the author to successfully gain admission to the University of California—San Diego. The fact that upon coming to America the writer enjoyed the beauty and salubriousness of San Diego so much readily accounts for the author's concurrence with San Diego's moniker as "America's finest city."

Under the principalship of Mr. Okodi, Chief Iyabode Akin-Olugbade's teachers at Baptist Academy included the legendary Chief S. L. Akintola, the Premier of the Western Region of Nigeria at the time of the coup d'état of January 15, 1966, and Rev. Dr. J. A. Adegbite. After secondary school, Chief Iyabode Akin-Olugbade graduated with a teaching certificate from Idi-Aba Baptist Girls Teacher Training College in Abeokuta. Upon completing her studies, she started teaching at Ade-Oshodi Memorial Baptist School, Oke-Popo, Lagos.

Chief Iyabode Akin-Olugbade married Chief Ohu Akin-Olugbade on January 10, 1946. She taught for five years, until 1951, and then joined her husband in London, England. While in London, Mrs. Akin-Olugbade obtained her advanced teacher's certificate. She returned to Nigeria in December 1953 and again taught at Ade-Oshodi Memorial Baptist School and became a leader of the First Baptist Church, Lagos.

In 1958, Chief Iyabode Akin-Olugbade left Lagos for Ibadan, where her husband had become the chairman of the Western Nigeria Finance Corporation in 1957. She was a stalwart supporter of her husband during the turbulent years of the First Republic from 1960 to 1967. She founded Ago-Egba Stores during the first military interregnum and was a director of Chief Ohu Akin-Olugbade's OBA Group of Companies. In 1977, she was conferred with the title of Otun Iyalode of Ago-Owu by the then Olowu of Owu, Oba Oyegbade.

Mrs. Akin-Olugbade was the mother of Mr. Olusunmade Akin-Olugbade, a chief executive officer; Dr. Bolu Akin-Olugbade, a lawyer and businessman; Dr. Segun Akin-Olugbade, a general counsel for the African Development Bank; and Dr. (Mrs.) Tolutope A. Bolawa, a medical practitioner.

Chief Iyabode Akin-Olugbade has been described as being accommodating; caring; devoted; generous; gentle; humble; resourceful; a good Christian, mother, and wife, yet strict when warranted; and the pedagogue of many prominent Nigerians. The author can recall her being known as Sister by relatives and friends. Chief Gladys Ibijoke Iyabode Akin-Olugbade was a very comforting and sympathetic confidante of the author's mother. She died in London on October 21, 1988.

———

Akin-Olugbade, Prince Olusunmade B. A. Personal Communication. February 21, 2008.

==

Chief Ohu Babatunde Akin-Olugbade

(January 15, 1913-November 11, 1987)

Ekerin of Egbaland, Balogun of Owu, and Entrepreneur

Chief Ohu Babatunde Akin-Olugbade was born on January 15, 1913, to Papa Ojeleye and Mama Ajibola Asunle, renowned and respected traders. Papa Ojeleye, who was born in 1880, was a healer and midwife while Mama Asunle was a trader who traveled regularly between Lagos and northern Nigeria. Since his mother traveled so frequently, Chief Ohu Akin-Olugbade was raised by his stepmother until his father's death in 1922 when his mother became a more consistent influence. Chief O. B. Akin-Olugbade's royal pedigree extends to his third-generation paternal grandfather who was Oba Alaiyeluwa Arowayo of Orile-Owu. As his mother was a Muslim, Ohu was encouraged to learn the Koran. The Baptist mission in Abeokuta later converted the Olugbade family to Christianity, and Ohu was converted to Christianity in 1925. Young Ohu attended elementary school at the Owu Baptist Day School, Abeokuta, for three years. He then transferred to Baptist Boys High School, Abeokuta, from 1926 to 1931. Here he did the menial work reserved for all freshmen, including fetching firewood, cutting grass, drawing well water, washing plates, and cleaning toilets. He excelled in such subjects as arithmetic, English language, and religious knowledge and showed an aptitude for debating, which was a good foundation for his legal career. He loved sports, excelling as a swimmer (from his days on the banks of the Ogun River), a high jumper, and a member of the school's soccer team.

Chief Ohu Akin-Olugbade married Miss Iyabode Abati-George on January 10, 1946. He then proceeded to England in 1950 to study law and was called to the Bar at Lincoln's Inn in 1953. He returned to Nigeria in the same year and started his law practice with the then chief magistrate Lapite at 14 Tinubu Street, Lagos. In 1954, he set up his own chambers at 13/15 Balogun Street, Lagos. His chambers have spawned such legal luminaries as former attorney-general, and minister of justice, Prince Bola Ajibola; Chief Bayo Kehinde, SAN; Mrs. A. Akerele; and former chief magistrate Adeniran Adepegba, who were all tyros there at some point in their careers. Chief Akin-Olugbade was blessed with thirteen children, including Mr. Olusunmade Akin-Olugbade, a chief executive officer; Dr. Bolu Akin-Olugbade, a lawyer and businessman; Dr Segun Akin-Olugbade, a general counsel for the African Development Bank; and Dr. (Mrs.) Tolutope A. Bolawa, a medical practitioner.

Chief O. B. Akin-Olugbade entered into business by establishing the companies listed below, following the January 15, 1966, coup and the abrogation of political activities until 1978:

1971	Akin-Olugbade Hospital
1971	Niger Oil Resources Company
1973	OBA Transport
1973	OBA Property
1973	OBA International

1973	OBA Travels
1973	OBA Jewelers / AG Tabet
1974	ARC Nigeria—a Lagos company specializing in road construction, road surfacing, and civil engineering
1981	Akin-Olugbade Social Centre, Owu
1981	Nigeria Political and Research Bureau, Abeokuta

The Niger Oil Resources Company represents a breakthrough in the indigenization process of the Nigerian economy following independence. Chief Ohu Akin-Olugbade was the most successful of the four original entrepreneurs who were awarded oil exploration grants, namely J. O. K. Amakri, Henry Oluyede Majemirokun, and S. L. Edu. Other companies in which Chief Ohu Akin-Olugbade had interests are Management Enterprises, Marine and General Assurance Company, and Industrial Cartons

Politically, Chief Ohu Akin-Olugbade's first foray into affairs of state was as a member of the Nigerian Youth Movement from 1946 to 1950. The Nigerian Youth Movement was the second nationalist political party in Nigeria after Herbert Macaulay's Nigerian National Democratic Party founded in 1923. As a qualified attorney, Chief O. B. Akin-Olugbade joined Chief Obafemi Awolowo's Action Group and was very actively involved in its machinations. Chief Ohu Akin-Olugbade became chairman of the Western Nigeria Finance Corporation on November 4, 1957, following the elevation of Chief S. L. Akintola as the federal minister of communications and aviation in August of that year. In the 1959 federal general elections, Attorney Akin-Olugbade won his Egba south federal constituency by a landslide; but despite its more sophisticated campaign, the Action Group became the opposition party to the NPC-NCNC coalition in Lagos. The Northern People's Congress (NPC) represented northern Nigeria for the most part. National Convention of Nigerian Citizens, later known as the National Council of Nigeria and the Cameroons (NCNC) had its political base in, and represented, eastern Nigeria. From 1959 to 1963, Chief Ohu Akin-Olugbade was the chief whip in the Federal House of Representatives. After Chief Obafemi Awolowo was indicted for treasonable felony in 1963, Chief O. B. Akin-Olugbade became the leader of the opposition, contributing to the peace and stability of Nigeria, particularly in the areas of education, external affairs, and health.

Nigeria gained independence from England on October 1, 1960, and Dr. Nnamdi Azikiwe was declared the first indigenous Governor-General of the country. In 1963, Nigeria became a republic, and Dr. Nnamdi Azikiwe became the first president of the country while Alhaji Tafawa Balewa was the prime minister. In the ensuing federal general elections of 1964, Chief O. B. Akin-Olugbade again won his seat, representing the newly constituted coalition of southern parties—which consisted of the AG, NCNC, NEPU, and UMBC—the United Progressive Grand Alliance (UPGA). They again formed the loyal opposition to the northern union, the Nigeria National Alliance (NNA), comprised of the NPC and the NNDP. Chief Akin-Olugbade was the leader of the opposition. Chief Ohu Akin-Olugbade remained active in politics until his death.

Chief Akin-Olugbade's fiscal responsibility was amply demonstrated by the manner in which he sailed through the proceedings of the Coker Commission without reproach. According to the terms of reference contained in the official *Federal Government Gazette* no. 47, vol. 49 of June16, 1962, the Coker Commission "was to enquire into the following matters, i.e.,:

(a) The financial and investment policies and practices, the management (including staff matters and staff regulations), and the business operations of each of the following statutory corporations since 1st October, 1954:

   (i)   The Western Region Marketing Board;
   (ii) The Western Nigeria Development Corporation
   (iii) The Western Region Finance Corporation
   (iv) The Western Region Housing Corporation
   (v)   The Western Nigeria Government Broadcasting Corporation
   (vi) The Western Nigeria Printing Corporation."

The Coker Commission of Inquiry into the activities of the Western Region Finance Corporation from 1954 to 1962 proved to be a very controversial panel. Chief S. L. Akintola was the chairman of the Western Region Finance Corporation from 1955 to 1957, followed, from 1957 to 1959, by Chief Akin-Olugbade. He, in turn, was succeeded in 1960 by Chief Babalola. Despite its avowed aim, the Coker Commission did not find any shenanigans, or malpractice, on the part of Chief Ohu Akin-Olugbade during his tenure as chairman of the Western Region Finance Corporation. All the unsubstantiated accusations leveled by the Coker Commission rolled off Chief Akin-Olugbade as if he were indeed covered with veritable teflon coating.

Although he regarded himself as a citizen of the world, Chief Akin-Olugbade received many honors from his hometown. In 1958, he received the prestigious and cherished title of Are-Ona-Kakanfo of Owu. In 1976, Chief Akin-Olugbade was bestowed with the tile of Balogun of Owu. In 1977, the even more revered title of ekerin of Egbaland was conferred upon him. In order to hold the titles that Chief Akin-Olugbade dignified, one must be a man of demonstrated honesty, intelligence, personableness, good character, high reputation, community orientation, and traditional values. The title of Are-Ona-Kakanfo recalls the military days of the Yoruba when that title personified the feared commander in chief of the army whose position it was to continually enlarge the Yoruba Empire. Traditionally, a Balogun was a preeminent war chief. The title has retained its high profile, and elevated status, into contemporary times. As a kingmaker, a Balogun must now maintain the customs and traditions of the people whom he represents while simultaneously espousing their anomie and prosperity. An Ekerin of Egbaland, the fourth in line to the throne, is a member of the Alake's cabinet representing the people of Owu. The Ekerin of Egbaland might serve as a member of the Alake's suite or, upon request, personate him at any ceremony or function.

Another type of accolade for Chief Akin-Olugbade came by way of a song that was written for and about him. It may be rendered as follows:

ITOKU	ITOKU
Itoku mo jowuro	Itoku clearer than morning.
Omo onile ori oke	Offspring of the owner of house on hilltop
Ti nri a fomo eiye	Who sees the birds' little ones. Offspring of
Omo a f'ile p'ogun	the one who beats the drum of conspiracy.
Omo a luf'ote ja	Around Ladugbo quarters.
Ladugbu oforon	T'ewogbade adubodi.
T'ewogbade adubodi	Offspring of one who abuses with sharp
Omo oju bu ni sin enu Omo	tongue.
asa kankan l'ewa	Offspring of the cultured beauty pageant.

IWO	IWO
Omo Ara Iwo	Offspring of two indigenes of Oba River
Omo Odo Oba	The prince of Elemere
Omo Oba T'elumere Iwo	Iwo has neither doors
o ni lekun	Nor keys
Beni ko ni kokoro	The young slaves keep watch
Eru wewe l'amu d'ele	One who procures bravery with money
M'owo rakin	One who prefers bravery to cowardice
Omo ara `kin kofo r'ojo	Iwo, who plucks kola nut for festivals Iwo,
Iwo a k'abi soro	Iwo, Iwo
Iwo, Iwo, Iwo	Which the bird called
Ti o didere pe	And its peak got bent.
Tenu k'ako	

OWU	OWU.
Omo Olowu Oduru Omo l'agbo `are	Offspring of Olowu Oduru.
Omo Ajibosin	Offspring of the community leader.
Omo are ma tayi	Offspring of Ajibosin.
N'ibi omo eso po jomidan lo	Offspring of the resolute leaders
Omo asunkungbade	Where the soldiers outnumber the maidens.
Omo onileta b'isu	Offspring of those who snatch the crown amidst the tears.
Ohu	Offspring of the one who vibrates like yam in its heap.
Akehin okunrin l'ogun	Ohu, the last man in the battle.
Atotileto omo Akintunde	Renowned organizer.
	Offspring of Akintunde.

The translation of this song was made difficult because there are no accents on the words to indicate the tone and meaning of the piece.

On a whimsical note, although many may have repeated the aphorism, it was Chief O. B. Akin-Olugbade who first described two-door automobiles to the author as "get out so that I can get in" (so-kin-so) cars. Moreover, perhaps the author's most endearing story about Chief O. B. Akin-Olugbade is a pithy one, engendered when the author visited Chief Akin-Olugbade at his palatial home in Yaba, Lagos, shortly after a cousin of the author had graduated from law school. Unsolicited, Chief O. B. Akin-Olugbade asked the author's cousin whether or not he had purchased his lawyer's wig to be worn in court. When the author's cousin responded in the negative, Chief O. B. Akin-Olugbade immediately produced enough cash to cover the cost of a brand-new wig, self-assured in the knowledge that the author's cousin could not attend his law school graduation ceremonies without a lawyer's wig. That act of generosity amply encapsulated for the author the depth of caring and empathy that Chief O. B. Akin-Olugbade exhibited continuously toward his family and those close to him.

Chief Ohu Akin-Olugbade was a man who personified many virtues, including truthfulness, forthrightness, great listening skills, empathy, generosity, optimism, buoyancy, charisma, and being unrelentingly altruistic and honest. He was always willing to assist his employees and even built houses for them. By establishing his companies, he provided employment specifically for many Egba sons and daughters. Chief Ohu Babatunde Akin-Olugbade was an ideal husband and father who lavished affection on his wife, children, and relatives. The twentieth anniversary observance of Chief Akin-Olugbade's death was held at the Abeokuta Memorial Hall on Sunday, November 4, 2007. It was a befitting ceremony for one who is beloved and remembered for his philanthropy and largess, not only in Abeokuta and Lagos, but also throughout the Nigerian Diaspora.

Akin-Olugbade, Prince Olusunmade B. A. Personal Communication. February 21, 2008.

===

Prince Olusunmade Babajimi Aremu Akin-Olugbade

(March 24, 1950—)

Entrepreneur

Born in Lagos, Nigeria, Prince Sunmade Akin-Olugbade of the Atileta Ruling House of Owu, Abeokuta, Nigeria, may be described as a man with intercontinental perspicuity—a proficiency honed via extensive travel in the United States of America, South Korea, and various countries in Europe. He is at ease in many countries of the world with equal facility. Prince Sunmade's father was the late Chief Honorable Ohu Babatunde Akin-Olugbade, the former Balogun of Owu and the ekerin Alake of Abeokuta. His mother was the late Chief Gladys Ibijoke Iyabode Akin-Olugbade, the former otun iyalode of Ago-Owu. Prince Sunmade has three siblings: two brothers—Bolu Akin-Olugbade, Ph.D., an attorney and businessman, and Adesegun Akin-Olugbade, Ph.D., general counsel for the African Development Bank—and a sister, Dr. Tolutope A. Bolawa, a medical practitioner. A beacon as a devoted family man, Prince Sunmade has been blessed with three sons: Akinkunmi, Akinbomi, and Oluwasegun. A highly numinous man, Prince Sunmade is on the board of trustees of the Israel Baptist Church

==

Fela Anikulapo-Kuti

(1938-August 1997)

Musician, Political Activist

Fela Anikulapo-Kuti, known simply as Fela, developed the Afro-beat form of music, which is a combination of American jazz, soul music, and Nigerian highlife music. His lyrics were highly critical of contemporary politicians. He was exiled to Ghana from 1978 to 1980 and was sentenced to five years in prison in 1985 but released in 1986 because of public protests.

With a large band of close to forty musicians and dancers, his first nightclub in Lagos, Kakadu, on Hughes Avenue (Agege Motor Road) was the main venue of his successful concerts and talk shows.

> Fela Anikulapo-Kuti, previously Ransome-Kuti in honor of his mother, Chief Olufunmilayo Ransome-Kuti, was born in Abeokuta, Nigeria, in 1938 . . . His father, Reverend Israel Oludotun Ransome-Kuti, like his grandfather, was a minister of the Protestant church, and director of the local grammar school. His mother was a teacher, but later became a politician of some considerable influence. As a teenager, Fela would run for miles to

attend traditional celebrations in the area, already feeling that the authentic African culture of his ancestors ought to be preserved.

His parents sent him to London in 1958, but rather than study medicine like his brothers and sister, Fela chose to register at the Trinity School of Music, where he was to spend the next five years. Whilst still a student, he married a [Yoruba] girl named Remi and had three children. In his spare time, Fela formed his first musical group, Koola Lobitos in 1959 with other Nigerian musicians living in London. Among these was J. K. Bremah, who had previously influenced Fela by introducing him to African music circles in Lagos at a time when Western music predominated there.

Fela returned to the Nigerian capital in 1963, three years after independence. Soon after, he was playing highlife and jazz, fronting the band with those of the musicians who had come back from England.

Over the next few years they performed regularly in Lagos and then in 1969, in the midst of the Biafra War, Fela decided to take Koola Lobitos to the United States. In Los Angeles, he changed the name of the group to Fela Ransome-Kuti and Nigeria 70.

At the club where they were playing, he met an African American girl, Sandra Isodore, who was a close friend to the Black Panthers. She introduced Fela to the philosophy and writings of Malcolm X, Eldridge Cleaver and other Black activists and thinkers, through which he was to become aware of the link existing between Black people all over the world. Through this insight, Fela also gained a clearer understanding of his mother's fight for the rights of Africans under colonial rule in Nigeria, together with her support of the pan-Africanist doctrine expounded by Kwame Nkrumah, the Ghanaian Head of State, who had negotiated independence for his country with the British.

Whilst in Los Angeles, Fela also found the inspiration he was seeking to create his own unique style of music, which he named Afro-beat. Before leaving America, the band recorded some of these new songs. Back at home, Fela once again changed the name of his group, this time to Fela Ransome-Kuti & Africa 70. The L. A. recordings were released as a series of singles.

The new African music was a great success in Lagos and Fela was to open a club in the Empire Hotel, called Afro-Shrine. At that time he was still playing the trumpet, having not yet hanged to the saxophone and piano. He started singing in mostly Pidgin English rather than in Yoruba, so as to be understood all over Nigeria and in the neighborhood countries. In his songs, he depicted everyday social situations with which a large part of the African population were able to identify.

Young people from all over Nigeria flocked to hear his songs which developed themes relating to Blackism and Africanism, encouraging a return to traditional African religions. Later he was to become satirical and sarcastic towards those in power, condemning both military and civilian regimes for their crimes of mismanagement, incompetence, corruption, and marginalizing the underprivileged.

In 1974, pursuing his dream for an alternative society, he . . . declared his home to be an independent state: the Kalakuta Republic . . . He changed his name from "Ransome-Kuti" to "Anikulapo-Kuti" . . . His records began to sell in the millions. The population of the Kalakuta Republic grew amidst mounting criticism, particularly of the young people, many of whom were still in their teens, who left their families to live there.

During the "Festival for Black Arts and Culture" (FESTAC) held in Lagos in 1977, Fela sang Zombie, a satire against the military, which was to become enormously popular throughout Africa, bringing down the fury of the Nigerian army upon him and his followers. As Fela relates in Unknown Soldier, a thousand soldiers attacked the Kalakuta Republic, burning down his house and beating all of its occupants. The song tells that, during the course of this attack, his mother was thrown from a first-floor window and later died from her injuries.

Homeless and without a Shrine, which had also been destroyed along with the entire neighbourhood, Fela and his group moved to the Crossroads Hotel. A year later Fela went to Accra to arrange a tour. Upon his return, to mark the 1st Anniversary of the destruction of the Kalakuta Republic, Fela married twenty-seven girls in a collective ceremony, many of whom were his dancers and singers, giving them all the name of Anikulapo-Kuti. After the wedding, the whole group set off for Accra where concerts had been planned. In a packed Accra stadium, as Fela played Zombie, riots broke out. The entire group was arrested and held in custody for two days before being put on a plane bound for Lagos, banned from returning to Ghana.

Upon his return to Lagos, still with nowhere to live, Fela and his entire entourage squatted the offices of Decca, where they remained for almost two months. Soon after, Fela was invited, with the seventy-strong Africa 70, to play at the Berlin festival. After the show, almost all of the musicians ran away. Despite this catalogue of setbacks, Fela returned to Lagos determined to continue.

The King of Fro-beat and his Queens went to live in Ikeja, in J. K. Bremah's house: a new Kalakuta. There, Fela more political than ever, went on to form his own party, "Movement of the People." He presented himself as a Presidential candidate in the 1979 elections that would return the country to civilian rule. His candidature was refused. Four years later, at the next elections, Fela once again tried to become president . . .

In 1984, . . . Fela served a two-year prison sentence on currency charges . . .

Considering himself to be the spiritual son of Kwame Nkrumah, the renowned Ghanaian pan-Africanist, Fela Anikulapo-Kuti was a violent critic of colonialism and neocolonialism. Over the past twenty years, he became famous as a spokesman for the great mass of people, in Nigeria and elsewhere in Africa and the African Diaspora, disenchanted with the period of post independence.

His sad death in August 1997 was mourned by the nation. Even those who did not agree with him were among the million people or more who attended his funeral. Even the many governmental letters of condolence sent to his family were eloquent testimonials to a great man. His death was attributed to AIDS-related causes, though a more popular diagnosis was that his system was sufficiently weakened by the countless beatings at the hands of the authorities so as to allow disease to enter.

Throughout his life, Fela was sustained by the unconditional love and respect offered to him by the millions of people whose lives he touched. In death he retains the legendary status by which he was proclaimed by the throngs of people who came to pay their last respects at his laying in state in Tafawa Balewa Square "Abami Eda" (Chief Priest). "He will live forever."

Stein, Rikki (London). Insert in *Fela and Africa 70: Sorrow Tears and Blood*. Lagos, Nigeria: Fama Press Nigeria Co, 1977.

<http://incolor.inetnebr.com/cvanpelt/felaweb/africaman.html>
    Retrieved January 21, 2004

<http://kalakutarepublic.free.fr/english/biography.htm>
    Retrieved January 21, 2004

<http://www.newmuseum.org/now_cur_fela.php>
    Retrieved January 21, 2004

===

Dr. Saburi Oladeni Biobaku

(June 16, 1918-2001)

Educator, Author, and Administrator

Professor Biobaku was born in Igbore, Abeokuta, on June 16, 1918, to the family of a prominent Muslim Oba and wealthy businessman. He was educated at Ogbe Methodist Primary School, Abeokuta; Government College, Ibadan; and Higher College, Yaba. He graduated from the University of Exeter, England, with a bachelor's degree in history in 1945 and earned a second bachelor's degree, this time in English, from Trinity College, Cambridge, in 1947. He obtained his master's degree from Cambridge University. He then earned his doctorate in history from the University of London's Institute of Historical Research in 1950. Between 1951 and 1957, he was the assistant liaison officer for Nigerian students in the United Kingdom. Upon returning to Nigeria, he taught high school at his alma mater—Government College, Ibadan—for a while. Dr. Biobaku later became the secretary to the Premier of the Western Region of Nigeria. From 1953 to 1957, Dr. Biobaku held the position of Registrar of the University College of Ibadan. In 1961, he was the professor of history at the University of Ife. In 1964, Dr. Biobaku reached the apogee of university administration when he was appointed as the first Vice-Chancellor of the University of Lagos. Professor Biobaku has also served as the vice president of the Society of African Universities, as well as the chairman of the Nigerian National Antiques Commission, the Nigerian Textile Mills corporation, and on the editorial board of the Encyclopedia Africana.

Dr. Biobaku has written many scholarly books that are putatively influential standards in African history, including the 1957 publication of his dissertation, his ninety-nine-page opus: *The Egba and Their Neighbours, 1842-1872*. In 1973, Dr. Biobaku published another superordinate book: *Sources of Yoruba History.*

Hermeneutically, Dr. Biobaku opined that Pan-Africanism should foster and nurture the health, wealth, and literacy of individual personalities within Africa to ensure that the hard-won liberties of independence would be used to ride the wave of upward mobility for everyone. To this end, he supported the creation and utilization of regional organizations within Africa in order to consummate economic and social goals. He was also a strong advocate of Yoruba unity. In consonance with the perspective of this book, Professor Biobaku was an adherent of a four-tiered political structure for Nigeria that would encompass federal, regional, state, and local administrations.

Professor Biobaku was the vice-chancellor of the University of Lagos while the author attended that institution. Chief Biobaku's chauffeur at the time was a cousin of the author's and a point of entrée and acquaintance. Unfortunately, it was during this period that Dr. Biobaku was stabbed in the back by a student radical who believed that Professor Biobaku had been unfairly named to the vice-chancellery. Dr. Biobaku survived the attack. Dr. Biobaku was married and is survived by one child.

Osso, Nyakano. ed. *Newswatch Who's Who in Nigeria.* Lagos: Newswatch Communications Limited, 1990.

<http://en.wikipedia.org/wiki/Saburi_Biobaku>
    Retrieved November 13, 2009.

==

Bishop Samuel Ajayi Crowther

(1809-1891)

First African Bishop of the Anglican Church

Samuel Ajayi Crowther was born in Osogu, western Nigeria. He was born during the period of the demise of the Old Oyo Empire and the establishment of the Fulani Empire of Usman dan Fodio. Consequently, warfare and slave raiding were endemic. Young Ajayi was captured in 1821 by marauding Yoruba and Fulani armies and sold to Portuguese slave traders when Osogun was raided. Bishop Crowther later recorded the slaughter and desolation of the ordeal. In April 1822, the British Preventive Squadron intercepted the Portuguese ship that Crowther was on and disembarked him in Sierra Leone along with thousands of his shipmates. Sierra Leone was established as a Christian colony by the coteries of William Wilberforce, the English abolitionist, and the Clapham Sect. It was initially populated by manumitted slaves from the New World and, following the abolition of the slave trade by the British parliament in 1807, quickly became a base for the British Preventive Squadron mandated to freeing slaves who were being transported to the New World.

Acculturating to the lifestyle of Sierra Leone—including language, family names, clothing, education, religion, and buildings—Crowther was baptized in approximately 1825 by the Reverend John Rahan of the Church Missionary Society of England (CMS) and adopted the name of Samuel Crowther after a member of the CMS's home committee.

In 1827, the CMS founded Fourah Bay College as a Christian school, which would be the first institution to offer university education in West Africa. Crowther was one of its first students and later acquired a diploma. Serving as an interpreter in collaboration with the German missionary J. F. Schon, Crowther returned to Nigeria in 1841 as part of Sir Thomas Fowell Buxton's Niger expedition, designed to form an alliance of Westernizing, proselytizing, and entrepreneurial interests that would destroy the slave trade once and for all. Consequently, Crowther was ordained in 1844 and posted to Nigeria as a full-time missionary. It was at this time that Crowther began his literary career with the publication of a book on Yoruba vocabulary and grammar. Reconnoitering with the English missionary Henry Townsend as a co leader, along with a German missionary C. A. Gollmer, a large group of Sierra Leoneans decided to establish a mission in Abeokuta in 1846. Carpenters, builders, teachers, and catechists were determined to construct a mission in Abeokuta that would transplant their talents and way of life. The mission was responsible for extricating Abeokuta from the slave economy by introducing and growing cotton, establishing the Church Missionary Society, and ensuring the independence of Abeokuta from British consular administration. Upon being reunited with his mother and sister, Crowther ensured that they were among the first in Abeokuta to be baptized. As an evangelist, Crowther was the first African to transliterate an enduring version of the Bible into vernacular Yoruba—or any other African language.

Crowther's next successes came in the Nupe part of Nigeria. In 1857, under the sponsorship of McGregor Laird, J. C. Taylor, an Igbo, established a mission at Onisha while Crowther proceeded into Nupe territory, working with an entirely African force. In collaboration with Henry Venn, the head of the CMS, Crowther succeeded in reducing the Nupe language into writing. Crowther wrote the first book on Igbo as well as a premier dictionary of Hausa. In order to enhance communication among each other, Creole emerged as the lingua franca of the missionaries, thereby displacing the variegated languages spoken by disparate Sierra Leonean evangelists.

Crowther's master status was achieved in 1864, when Venn secured Crowther's consecration as bishop of "the countries of western Africa beyond the limits of the Queen's dominions." Although thus proscribed, Crowther's reticence about becoming a bishop was overcome because Venn insisted on developing an indigenous episcopate. After clashes with white missionaries over policies, he resigned in 1890. Bishop Crowther died of a stroke on December 31, 1891, a disconsolate and desolate man. Posthumously, the minutia of his ministry quickly unraveled as a European bishop succeeded him, and the indigenization of the episcopate ceased.

Nonetheless, Crowther's impeccable legacy is incontrovertible. Among his myriad attributes, his humility, integrity, graciousness, irenicism, and piousness are nonpareil. His son, Dandeson, became an Anglican archdeacon; and his son-in-law, T. B. Macaulay, became a principal of Lagos Grammar School. Bishop Crowther received an honorary doctorate and is now considered an icon of the African church. He has a commemorative plaque in Westminister Abbey in London, England.

Curtin, Philip D. *Africa Remembered: Narratives by West Africans from the Era of the Slave Trade*, pp. 289-316. Madison: The University of Wisconsin Press, 1967.

Walls, Andrew F. *Samuel Ajayi Crowther (1807-1891)*, 1992.

===

Dr. Taslim Olawale Akanni Elias, Esq.

(November 11, 1914-August 13, 1991)

Jurist, Educator, Professor of Law

Judge Taslim Olawale Elias was a distinguished jurist, legal scholar, and administrator. He was called to the Bar in 1947 and was the first Nigerian to obtain a Ph.D. in law. He was a legal intellectual and fellow in different institutions before serving as Nigeria's attorney general and minister of justice from 1960 to 1972. Concomitantly, from 1966 to 1972, he was also a professor of law and dean of the Faculty of Law at the University of Lagos. Dr. Elias was the chief justice of Nigeria from 1972 to 1975. In 1975, he was appointed to the International Court of Justice at The Hague and later served as the president of the court. Judge Elias was a member of the International Court at The Hague until his death in 1991. Judge Elias served in various other important capacities, received many honorary doctorates, and published several influential legal studies. The author is proud to trumpet the fact that Justice Elias and he attended the same high school-Igbobi College. Justice Taslim Elias was truly a colossus of the law.

Ample testimony as to the illustriousness of Judge Elias is provided by the fact that the following list of dignitaries either attended his interment or forwarded messages of condolences:

> Her Majesty, Beatrix, Queen of the Netherlands;
> His Majesty King Hussein Bin Tolal I of Jordan; the Right Honorable Lord Denning; the prime minister of Dominica, Engenia Charles;
> His Excellency, Mr. Javier Perez de Cuellar, former secretary-general of the United Nations, and other top officials of the United Nations;
> the president, present and former members, present and former registrars, deputy registrars, and the entire members of staff of the International Court of Justice;
> the president and members of the curatorium of the Hague Academy of International Law;
> the president and members of the Institute de Droit International;
> Honorable minister of external affairs of the Federal Republic of Nigeria;
> His Eminence, the Sultan of Sokoto, Alhaji Ibrahim Dasuki;
> His Royal Highness, the Oba of Lagos;
> His Royal Highness, the Oba of Benin;
> His Royal Highness, the Oni of Ife;
> Honorable chief justice of Nigeria;
> Honorable justices and the registrar of the supreme court and their spouses;

the Honorable president of the court of appeals and judges of the
court of appeals and their spouses;

members of the federal and state executive councils;

the Board of Trustees of the Taslim Elias Chair of Jurisprudence
and International Law at the University of Lagos;

the chairman, officers, and members of the Nigerian Society of
International Law;

the former attorney general of the Federation of Nigeria, and
Minister of Justice, Prince Bola Ajibola, and the entire
professional and administrative staff of the Federal Ministry
of Justice;

foremost and eminent Nigerians from all walks of life;

the chairman and entire staff of St. Nicholas Hospital;

entire university communities, including chairmen of council,
senate, vice-chancellors, and their deputies, registrars,
teaching and administrative staff—especially of Lagos,
Ibadan, Ife, ABU, Nsukka, and Abuja, and most particularly
of Lagos State University;

the director, secretary, and staff of the Nigerian Law School;

members of the Diplomatic Corps—particularly Sir Christopher
Macrea, of the United Kingdom and J. T. W. Kwint, of the
Netherlands—of Japan and the Arab Republic of Egypt;

the dean and professors of the Faculty of Law, University of
Hull;

Professor Antony Allott and numerous distinguished friends and
colleagues at home and abroad;

the Baba Adinni of Nigeria and the Lagos Central Mosque;

the Ansar-Ud-Deen Society of Nigeria;

the Muslim Association of Nigeria, Isale-Eko;

the officers and members of the Isale-Eko Descendant's Union;

the Council of Lagos State Indigenes;

the Egbe Omo Eko;

former military and civilian governors and secretaries to their
governments;

former secretaries to the federal military government;

former chief justices of Nigeria and justices of the federal and
states' judiciary and their spouses;

senior advocates of Nigeria and members of the Nigeria Bar
Association;

old boys, principal, staff, and pupils of Igbobi College, Yaba; veteran and present-day gentlemen of the press; and myriads of friends, admirers and well-wishers.

––––––

The Nigerian *Daily Times*, Thursday, August 13, 1992, p. 32.

==

Alaiyeluwa, Alake Gbadebo I

(June 1854-May 28, 1920)

The Sixth Alake of Abeokuta

Oba Gbadebo I was born in 1854. This was at a time when his father, Oba Okukenu, the first Alake of Abeokuta, was searching for the head of Oba Okikilu, his predecessor. Oba Okukenu wanted his predecessor's skull so that he could use it in propitiation ceremonies upon his accession to the Alakeship. He ruled from 1898 to 1920.

==

Alaiyeluwa, Alake Samuel Adesina Gbadebo II

The Eighth Alake of Abeokuta

Oba Gbadebo II was the paramount ruler of Egbaland from September 29, 1963, to 1971. Oba Gbadebo II was from the Laarun Ruling House.

==

Alaiyeluwa, Alake Michael Adedotun Aremu Gbadebo III

(September 4, 1943—)

The Tenth Alake of Abeokuta

Oba Michael Adedotun Aremu Gbadebo III was born on September 14, 1943. He is a grandson of Oba Gbadebo I and a nephew of Oba Adesina Gbadebo II.

Oba Gbadebo III is one of the six children of Omoba Adesanya Osolake Gbadebo and Madam Amoke Gbadebo, a distinguished Egba woman from the Ikopa area of Abeokuta. He is married to Dr. Tokunbo Gbadebo, who is the daughter of Chief J. F. Odunjo, the legendary Yoruba novelist and author of the popular Alawiye book series. They have four sons, who are successful professionals.

The year 1943, as the year of Oba Gbadebo III's birth, is propitious in Egba history because it marked the centennial anniversary of the advent of Christianity to Egbaland. Abeokuta is the site of not only the first church in Nigeria, but also the first church in West Africa. The churches taught literacy as well as religion. This fact has had the effect of providing the Egba with a legacy of erudition that has propelled them into the professions earlier than the residents of any other part of Nigeria.

Prior to the announcement of his appointment as the Alake of Abeokuta, Prince Gbadebo enjoyed a successful career in the Nigerian Army. He rose to be a principal staff officer to the chief of staff, Supreme Headquarters, Major General Tunde Idiagbon from January 1984 to September 1985 and retired from the army as a colonel. He has been awarded such military honors as the National Service Medal (NSM), the Defense Service Medal, and the Forces Service Star (FSS) Medal. He joined the board of the oil company Oando PLC in April 2006 and has served on the boards of several other companies, including Global Haulage Resources. He is an alumnus of the famous Baptist Boys High School, Abeokuta. Gbadebo earned a Bachelor of Arts degree, and a graduate diploma, from the University of Ibadan, Nigeria's premier university.

Oba Gbadebo's election on August 3, 2005, as the Alake of Abeokuta ended six months of jostling for prominence by Egba sons who wished to succeed Oba Oyebade Lipede, who died on February 3, 2005. The aspirants included Gbadebo's younger brother, Adeleke; a United States-based businessman, Prince Olufemi Obadimu; and a property consultant, Prince Adedayo Shyllon-Sogbolu. Following propitiation ceremonies with the Ifa Oracle, which picked Prince Gbadebo, the announcement was made by the chairman of the Egba Alake kingmakers, Oba Adeyemi Adeboye, the Olowu of Egbaland, and independently concurred with by Oba Alani Bankole, the Olowu of Iporo. Oba Gbadebo is from the Laarun Ruling House. The election was ultimately confirmed by Governor Gbenga Daniel of Ogun State.

A devout Christian, Oba Adedotun Gbadebo considers the family to be the fountain and succor of a better society. He is regarded as being handsome, debonair, and a devoted public servant.

———

<file:///F:\ABEOKUTA\RegnantAlake.htm>
    Retrieved September 16, 2009.

<http://nigeriaworld.com/articles/2007/aug/243.html>
    Retrieved September 18, 2009.

<http://nm.onlinenigeria.com/templates/?a=4288&z=12>
    Retrieved September 18, 2009.

<http://www.egbaewa.org/Alake.htm>
    Retrieved September 18, 2009.

==

Chief John Akinwunmi George

(June 24, 1932—)

Insurance Entrepreneur, Chamber of Commerce Advocate

Chief John Akinwunmi George was born on June 24, 1932, to the late Chief (deacon) James Adeboye George and Chief (Mrs.) Elizabeth Ibidapo George. Chief Akin George graduated from Baptist Academy in Lagos in 1953. Following a short stint as a clerk for the Bank of British West Africa (now First Bank of Nigeria PLC), he switched from banking to insurance. Thus, in 1954, he joined the Royal Exchange Assurance Company, and remained with them until 1956 when he left for England. Between 1957 and 1960, he acquired experience by working as a clerk for three London companies: the Dominion Insurance Company, Willis Fabers Insurance Brokers, and B. D. Cooke and Partners. In 1960, he graduated from the College of Insurance, London. Upon graduation, he became an associate of the Chartered Insurance Institute (ACII) in 1961 and an associate of insurance brokers (ACIB) in 1962. He buttressed his position in the insurance profession by becoming a fellow of the Corporation of Insurance Brokers (FCIB) in 1973 and a fellow of the Insurance Institute of Nigeria (FIN) in 1976.

Chief Akin George returned to Nigeria in 1960 and immediately established his first company, J. Akin George and Company—an incorporated insurance brokerage company. He also founded Sierra Leone Insurance Brokers, Freetown, Sierra Leone, in 1964; Marine and General Assurance Brokers, Accra, Ghana, in 1969; Marine and General Assurance Company, Lagos, also in 1969; and United Africa Insurance Brokers, London, in 1973. Currently, he is the chairman of these companies while serving as the executive chairman of the Marine and General Assurance Company, Lagos.

Chief John Akin George's greatest claim to fame is as an indefatigable proponent for chambers of commerce as well as for the various Nigerian and international trade associations of the insurance business. Using J. Akin George and Company as a vehicle, he joined the Lagos Chamber of Commerce and Industry in 1964; and via assiduous exertion, he became the president of the chamber in 1979. During his tenure, he was instrumental in the construction of Commerce House—the secretariat of the Lagos Chamber of Commerce at 1 Idowu Taylor Street, Victoria Island, Lagos.

In addition to serving as the president of the Insurance Institute of Nigeria in 1972 and 1982, Chief Akin George has held many other positions in various chambers of commerce:

a) Patron, Franco-Nigeria Chamber of Commerce;
b) Chairman, Nigeria / Korean Business Councils;
c) President, Nigerian Association of Chambers of Commerce, Industry, Mines and Agriculture (NACCIMA);
d) President, Nigeria Chamber of Commerce and Industry (LCCI);
e) Member of the executive council of the Federation of African Chamber of Commerce;
f) Member of the executive committee of the Nigeria-USA Business Councils;
g) Honorary general secretary and trustee of Nigeria-American Chambers of Commerce, 1964-1972;
h) President, Federation of West African Chambers of Commerce from 1990 to date.

In association with various colleagues, Chief Akin George has also established, and sits on the board of, companies in such variegated fields as banking, construction, brewing, hotel, and tourism. These institutions include the following:

1) Chairman, Akin and Bayo Investment and Industrial Company;
2) Chairman, JKN Construction Company;
3) Chairman, Nigerian Concrete Industries;
4) Chairman, Multimalt (Nigeria);
5) Chairman, Waldstan Nigeria;
6) Director, Fountain Trust Bank;
7) Founder, Ecobank, Lagos;

8) Vice president, Ecobank Transnational Incorporated, Lome, Togo;

9) Board member, Lagos Sheraton Hotel and Towers;

10) Board member, Marine Recoveries Services (Nigeria); and

11) Second vice president, Olabisi Onabanjo University Development Foundation (formerly the Ogun State University Development Foundation).

Over the years, Chief Akin George has earned several national and international honors and awards. In November 1982, in Ethiopia, he was honored with the Gold Mercury International Award for his contribution to production development as well as to cosmopolitan social and economic cooperation. On October 1, 1983, he was conferred with the national honor of the Officer of the Federal Republic (OFR) by the Federal Government of Nigeria in recognition of his contributions to the development of indigenous entrepreneurship and the economic progress of Nigeria. In 1996, he was also honored by the Commonwealth Institute of Journalism. Furthermore, his chieftaincy titles include the Babajiro of Ile-Oluji, Ondo State (1974); Lisa Ago Odo of Oke Ona, Abeokuta, Ogun State (1977); Bobagbimo of Egbaland, Ogun State (1979); and Ekweme of Assah Ubirielem by His Royal Highness, Eze Ebube G. O. Okwuakwa, Igwe II of Assah Ubirielem, Imo State (November 1990).

Socially, Chief Akin George belongs to many clubs. He is a member of the Apapa Club, Lagos; Island Club, Lagos; Metropolitan Club, Lagos; and Yoruba Tennis Club, Lagos; and he is a past president of the Lagos Rotary Club. Most importantly, he is a prominent member of the Baptist Convention. Chief Akin George is happily married with children.

A litany of virtues have been variously ascribed to Chief Akin George, including being dedicated; democratic; dignified; energetic; humble; loyal; patriotic; respectful; tactful; undogmatic; a consensus builder and strong negotiator; of good bearing; unfailingly graceful; unboundedly wise; zestful for a cause; devoted and patient in establishing, nursing, and harvesting the fruition of his business projects; a traditionalist in upholding Egba chieftaincy customs and culture while mixing easily with both young and old; and uncompromising on principles. He is perhaps delimited in that he is regarded by some as being blunt to a fault and overly sensitive to opposition.

George, John Akinwunmi. *Industrial and Economic Development in Nigeria: Selected Issues*, pp. xxiii-xxv.

===

Dr. Thomas Lambo (1929—)

Psychiatrist

Dr. Lambo was born in Abeokuta, trained as a psychiatrist in London, and began his active career in 1950 as a medical specialist for the Aro Hospital for Nervous Diseases in Lagos. He became a professor of psychiatry and dean of the medical faculty at the University of Ibadan in 1966, where he also became the college president in 1968. He was an international figure serving in various capacities, such as being the chairman of the West African Examinations council, founder and president of the Association of Psychiatrists in Africa, chairman of the Scientific Council for Africa (1965-1970), member of the executive committee of the Council for International Organization for Medical Science (UNESCO) from 1965 to 1968, chairman of the United Nations Advisory Committee for the Prevention of Crime and Treatment of Offenders (1968-1971), and assistant director general (and later deputy director) of the World Health Organization. Among his many awards are honorary doctorate degrees, membership of the Order of the British Empire, and the Selassie African Research Award for 1970.

The author spent many wonderful years with David, Dr. Lambo's son, during our carefree undergraduate days, exploring the nightlife, and indigenous mores of Ibadan. Also with us on those bucolic jaunts into the idyllic neighborhoods, amongst others, was A. Oladele Odimayo, the inimitable Lagos businessman and philanthropist.

Uwechue, Ralph. ed. *Africa Who's Who*. London: Africa Books Limited, 1991.

==

Alaiyeluwa, Alake Micheal Mofolorunso Oyebade Lipede

(January 26, 1915-February 3, 2005)

The Ninth Alake of Abeokuta

Alaiyeluwa, Oba Oyebade Lipede was the Alake of Abeokuta from 1915 to 2005. The essence of Alake Lipede's reign is aptly captured by Dr. Saburi Biobaku in a letter written on the occasion of the silver jubilee of the accession of Oba Lipede. Chief Biobaku's encomium read as follows:

> "Uneasy lies the head that wears the crown." "Egba soro sin" [the Egba are difficult to serve]. These are two sayings that come naturally to the Egba. Alayeluwa Oba (Dr.) Oyebade Lipede, the reigning Alake of the Egba, is fully aware of these himself and they constitute a challenge which he has cheerfully accepted. It is the hazard of his occupation, so to speak, but how well has he prepared for his immense responsibility as the undoubted leader of the Egba people.

To the British and to his critics, Macaulay appeared overbearing and crude. Macaulay saw himself as a nationalist, but due to two criminal convictions, he could not contest for elections and had to operate as a kingmaker. When Herbert Macaulay died in 1946, delegates came from many different parts of Nigeria, thus attesting to his widespread popularity. Herbert Macaulay's portrait used to be on a Nigerian currency bill.

Omololu, The Very Rev. Dr. 'Yinka. ed. *by the lagoon,* April/May 2006, vol. 8, no. 2, p. 30, Magazine of the Cathedral Church of Christ, Marina, Lagos.

Research Unit. ed. *Makers of Modern Africa: Profiles in History,* pp. 320-321. London: Africa Journal Limited for Africa Books Limited, 1981.

==

Dr. Moses Adekoyejo Majekodunmi

(August 1916—)

M. A. Majekodunmi was born in August 1916. He is the son of Chief James B. Majekodunmi, the Otun of the Egbas. He attended Abeokuta Grammar School, St. Gregory's College in Lagos, and the University of Dublin's Trinity College in Ireland where he graduated with a second-class honors degree in anatomy and physiology in 1936. In 1938 and 1940, he earned first-class honors degrees in bacteriology and clinical medicine from the same university. He completed his residency at National Children's Hospital, Dublin, in 1941 and at Rotunda Hospital, also in Dublin, from 1941 to 1942.

Dr. Majekodunmi returned to Nigeria in 1943. From 1949 to 1960, he was the senior specialist obstetrician and gynecologist for the Nigerian Federal Government Medical Services. He was also a consulting physician with Massey Street Maternity Hospital, Lagos; General Hospital, Lagos; and Creek Hospital, Lagos.

In the 1960s, he was a member of the Nigerian Senate. From 1961 to 1966, he was a federal minister of state for the army and, later, the federal minister of health during the First Republic. He was the founder and chairman of the Board of Governors of St. Nicholas Hospital, Lagos; chairman of the Egba

Maternity Clinic; board member with Westminster Dredging Company and Union Bank in Nigeria; and secretary of the Nigerian branch of the British Medical Association.

Domestically, he is a titled chief in both Lagos and Abeokuta but is perhaps best known for having been the Administrator of the Western Region in 1962 upon declaration of the state of emergency there. Internationally, he has held many prestigious positions, such as serving as the president of the sixteenth World Health Assembly in 1963 and the international vice president of the third World Conference on Medical Education in New Delhi in 1966.

He is a prolific author of several works, including a biography. He has seven children.

—————

<http://nigerianwiki.com/wiki/Moses_Majekodunmi>

==

General Olusegun Obasanjo

(March 5, 1937—)

Erstwhile President of Nigeria, Army General

Olusegun Obasanjo was born in Abeokuta, Ogun State, on March 5, 1937. He attended Abeokuta Baptist Boys High School.

was to be the online arm of the university as it sought to outstrip the confines of an urban institution and reach out to a mature student population.

A tangential appointment came in 1979 when Professor Olusanya was appointed as the director of studies of the National Institute for Policy and Strategic Studies to be located in Jos in Plateau State. The institute was intended to "provide a forum of intellectual and practical excellence for policy initiators and executors" (Olusanya, 2003: 117). Professor Olusanya left the institute prematurely in December 1981 because he felt that the principles of its founding fathers had been compromised by the appointment of a new director general, which had resulted in the abrogation of its ideal of becoming the premier center of excellence in the country with respect to articulating and forming national and international strategy and policy. However, this experience, with its attendant intellectual scope, was to be the harbinger of his appointment as the director general of the Nigerian Institute of International Affairs in Lagos.

Professor Olusanya was selected as the director general of the Nigerian Institute of International Affairs on April 17, 1984, because of his erudition and strength of character in the wake of his incumbent predecessor, Dr. Ibrahim Agboola Gambari, being appointed foreign minister and the acrimony that ensued thereafter. Established in 1961, by the 1980s, the Nigerian Institute of International Affairs had acquired an enhanced reputation as a think tank for international relations with Africa and the world. Dr. Olusanya was the director general of the Institute from 1984 to 1991.

At the completion of his tenure as the director general of the Nigerian Institute of International Affairs, Professor Olusanya was promoted within the ranks of foreign affairs personnel to become the ambassador extraordinary and plenipotentiary of Nigeria in France. The announcement was made in January 1991. Shortly afterward, on April 13, 1991, the Oni of Ife conferred upon Ambassador Olusanya the title of Obatunmise of Ife in recognition of his various contributions to national life. This was in augmentation of the Alake of Abeokuta, Oba Lipede, having laid the precedence in July 1989 by conferring upon Dr. Olusanya the title of Dagunja of Egbaland for meritorious services to the homeland. Ambassador Olusanya presented his letters of credence to President Francois Mitterrand of France on June 3, 1991, and he was thus thrust into a brand-new career, determined to do a consummate job as was his bent. Bureaucratically, two early achievements at the embassy were to raise morale by increasing salaries and, as with the Nigerian Institute of International Affairs, to computerize the operations of the mission.

Ambassador Olusanya also sought to extend Nigeria's visibility in France through the instrumentality of culture by arranging the first Franco-Nigerian Week from January 5-21, 1993. The event was very well received in Paris and featured variegated cultural, touristic, and economic aspects of Nigeria as well as the photographic, sculptural, musical, dance, video graphic, and movie arts of Nigeria. The upshot of the event was that Nigeria was not as easily confused with Niger—a Francophone country and neighbor of Nigeria—at least, by many in Paris, for a while thereafter. This heightened image for Nigeria was enhanced by the embassy's participation in all cultural events held in France during the tenure of Ambassador Olusanya, such as the first International Black Film Festival of 1994.

On August 29, 1995, Ambassador Olusanya received a cryptic telegram from the Ministry of External Affairs in Lagos recalling his appointment and informing him that he had to return to Lagos by September 29, 1995. Although he suspected why he was recalled, and whereas he was not given an official reason for this action by anyone in the Nigerian government, Ambassador Olusanya left Paris for Lagos on September 28, 1995—a day early. While, in retrospect, Ambassador Olusanya could speculate as to the events that portended his recall, he remains assured in the knowledge that during his tenure he had assuaged any lingering apprehensions that his hosts might have had about the rightful place of Nigeria in the comity of nations. He left Paris, and the Foreign Service, a fulfilled man.

Ambassador Olusanya's disillusionment with Nigeria, however, is that it remains a geographical expression waiting to become a great nation. Dr. Olusanya is married to Megan, and is blessed with five children who are successful in their own right: OlaOluwa, Bolanle, Folake, Jumoke, and Titilola. Laconically speaking, it is pertinent to note here that whilst still at the University of Lagos, Dr. Olusanya, in an avuncular gesture, introduced the author to the history of Abeokuta as being a worthy subject of study.

Olusanya, Gabriel. *Memoirs of a Disillusioned Patriot*. Ibadan, Nigeria: Oluseyi Press, 2003.

==

Chief Olufunmilayo Ransome-Kuti

(October 25, 1900-April 13, 1978)

Suffragette, Nationalist

Chief Olufunmilayo Ransome-Kuti was born and nurtured in Abeokuta. In 1919, she decided to study music and domestic science in England. Upon her return to Abeokuta, she worked as a schoolteacher before marrying the Reverend Israel Ransome-Kuti. Theirs was an autonomic, egalitarian marriage—an important consideration for the success of their union. An autonomic, egalitarian marriage is a marriage in which more or less equal numbers of separate decision areas are assigned to each partner (Savage, 1991: 107). She was an indefatigable suffragist and the leader of the anti-Alake Ademola II faction that led to the abdication of the Alake in 1948.

Mrs. Ransome-Kuti's fame rests partly on her mobilization of women in Abeokuta to ultimately establish the Egba Women's Union, which became a powerful political force. She served as the union's only president during her lifetime. Perhaps the Egba Women's Union's greatest success was as a result of their protest against the Alake of Abeokuta for enforcing trade regulations that were perceived as being adverse for female entrepreneurs. A consequence of this remonstration was that the Alake decided to abdicate in 1948, and reforms were introduced into the administration. Chief Ransome-Kuti was also active in the National Council of Nigeria and the Cameroons, serving as the only woman in the 1947 delegation to England in order to protest the Richards Constitution. She held various executive positions in the party.

Chief Kuti's biographers, Johnson-Odim and Mba, have provided us with an incisive physical and personal description of Chief Olufunmilayo Ransome-Kuti. They write, in part:

> Funmilayo Ransome-Kuti stood about five feet four inches tall and had a slender frame. Her high cheekbones and piercing gaze could be quite intimidating. She had a hearty laugh and a strong, clear voice that many informants concurred could be heard well even by a large crowd. She spoke rapidly, often gesticulating with her hands

when making a point, and displayed a great deal of passion in her speeches. Though many people commented that her manner could be brusque, they remember her as warm and concerned about people. In her role as a leader, she was able to capitalize on being simultaneously Western educated and grounded in tradition. The women looked up to her because of her education: the fact that she had been to England lent status and credibility to her role as their "representative" to the colonial government.

FRK was passionate about the women's struggle, and that passion sometimes elicited an autocratic leadership style, most especially from the other Western-educated members of the executive committee (though none resigned or provided any real opposition to her leadership). Diplomacy was not, in fact, her strong suit. In both public and private, her no-nonsense approach was not particularly tolerant of incompetence, dishonesty, pettiness, or disagreement, once she'd made up her mind. She listened to others, but she made up her own mind, and she took her role as leader seriously. The one thing of which she was never accused was wavering about what to do (Johnson-Odim and Mba: 76-77)

Chief Olufunmilayo Ransome-Kuti was venerated with an honorary doctorate degree and received Nigerian knighthood when she became a member of the Order of the Niger. She was also a recipient of the Lenin Peace Prize. Lady Ransome-Kuti was the mother of the popular Nigerian musician, Fela Anikulapo-Kuti, Professor Olikoyi Ransome-Kuti, and Dr. Beko Ransome-Kuti. Mrs. Kuti was the cousin of Oluwole Soyinka, the Nobel Prize winner for literature.

Johnson-Odim, Cheryl, and Nina Emma Mba. *For Women and the Nation: Fumilayo Ransome-Kuti of Nigeria*. Urbana and Chicago: University of Illinois Press, 1997.

==

Rev. Israel Oludotun Ransome-Kuti

(April 30, 1891-April 6, 1955)

Reverend, Nationalist

Rev. Israel Oludotun Ransome-Kuti was the husband of Chief Olufunmilayo Ransome-Kuti in a union that was characterized as being an autonomic, egalitarian marriage. This type of marriage may be defined as being one in which there is an approximate "balance of *relative* authority, however, the husband's and wife's ranges together are greater than the shared ranges" (Nixon: 221). Johnson-Odim and Mba, the biographers of Chief Olufunmilayo Ransome-Kuti have also provided a graphic description of Oludotun Ransome-Kuti. They elucidate, partly, by informing us that Oludotun Ransome-Kuti

> attended Gbagura Primary School and St. John's Primary School, Sunren Village, Ifo. In 1904, a visitor and friend of Oludotun's father [Rev. J. J. Ransome-Kuti], the Reverend (later Archdeacon) S. A. Delumo took a liking to Oludotun (as he was called) and asked for Rev. J. J. Ransome-Kuti's permission to take the child back to Lagos with him and enroll him in the CMS Grammar School there. Permission was granted. When the senior tutor of the CMS Grammar School, the Reverend M. S. Cole was invited to establish a grammar school in Abeokuta, Oludotun accompanied him and thus became the first pupil of the AGS. There he quickly completed his secondary education begun in Lagos.

> From 1909-12, Oludotun was a junior assistant teacher at the AGS which he then left to enroll at Fourah Bay College in Sierra Leone. From that college, he received his Bachelor of Arts degree in 1914. In 1915 he received his licentiate in theology from the University of Durham (England) through a program with Fourah Bay College, and in 1916 earned his first-class teacher's certificate (in 1940 he earned his master's degree from Durham through Fourah Bay). In 1916 he became an assistant master at the CMS Grammar School in Lagos, and in 1919 at just

twenty-seven, he was appointed principal of the Ijebu-Ode (a town quite near Abeokuta) Grammar School. (Johnson-Odim and Mba: 32-33)

The Reverend I. O. Ransome-Kuti was one of the founders of the Nigerian Union of Teachers (NUT) in the 1930s, the Nigerian Union of Students (NUS), the Nigerian arm of the West African Students Union (WASU), and the National Council of Nigeria and the Cameroons (NCNC) in 1944, as well as the Majeobaje Society in Abeokuta. He was sympathetic to the Nigerian Youth Movement (NYM) led by such luminaries of Nigerian history as Ernest Ikoli, Samuel Akinsanya, H. O. Davis, Nnamdi Azikiwe, and Obafemi Awolowo in the 1930s and 1940s. He was even tempered, jovial, fair, disciplined, patriotic, a Pan-Africanist, and had an evident capacity for learning.

==

Sir Josiah Akinbomi Savage, MON

(February 13, 1921-May 4, 2007)

Engineer

Sir Josiah Akinbomi Savage was born on February 13, 1921, at 68, Breadfruit Street in the heart of Lagos Island to the well-known and illustrious Savage family. His parents were Emmanuel Akinniyi Savage, the youngest in his family, and Mrs. Lucrecia Adetoun Savage, née Meredith. Emmanuel Akinniyi Savage was the author's grandfather and namesake, and he died in 1929.

Sir Akinbomi Savage's siblings were Mrs. Eugenia Remilekun Reis, Mrs. Gertrude Adeyemi Finnih, Mr. Fortunatus Akintunde Savage, and Mrs. Otolorin Olowu, all now deceased. Papa, as he was affectionately referred to, was, if you will, the last of the flock. The family was raised in a Christian household. Sir Akinbomi Savage was a chorister at St. Paul's Breadfruit Church, Lagos, under the organist, Mr. Luke Johnson, and his assistant, Mr. Emmanuel Adekunle Meadows. St. Paul's is an Anglican, Christian church.

Papa's primary education was at Mrs. Gipson's Primary School along the Marina, Lagos. In 1929, he attended CMS Grammar School, Lagos. The Church Missionary Society (CMS) was an Anglican missionary group that was very active in proselytizing southern Nigeria. Papa recalled that two of his elementary school classmates were Victor Babs Kayode and Bashiru Augusto. Between 1929 and 1934, other names accrued as classmates. They were Dayo Adeseye, Samuel Johnson, Ayo May, Otolorin Seton, Frances Ajayi Williams, Sadeko, T. A. Bank-Oki, Gbenro Wilson, Victor Hafner, Adeolu Allen, and Oluremi Agbebi.

At the end of 1935, the author's father left CMS Grammar School in the eighth grade to resume his studies at St. Gregory's College, Obalende, Lagos. His schoolmates there, among others, were Mr. T. A. Bank-Oki, Late Kehinde and Taiwo Sikuade, Late Dr. Abayomi Marinho, Edward Akin Doherty, Fela Young, Dr. Tunji Cole, Samuel Johnson, Bankole Beckley, Late Adio Moses, Francis Adeyi-Williams, Victor Haphner, and Dr. Harold Sodipo. They were joined in the ninth grade by Frederick Hughes, Robert Abiola Orisagunon, Morris Ojulari, Oladehinde Oso, J. O. Lowery, and Messrs. Coker and Cole. He also made acquaintances with students from Methodist Boys High School, and King's College, Lagos, including Edward Akin Doherty, Henry Ominiya, Kehinde and Taiwo Sikuade, Eko Macaulay, and Dr. Ewa. In 1936, students from CMS Grammar School combined with students from Methodist Boys High School, Lagos, and founded Igbobi College as a high school mostly for boarders.

In 1939, Papa started working for the Chemistry Department in the Ministry of Water Works, Lagos. After intensive training, he was transferred to Port

Harcourt, the capital of the present Rivers State, to establish a subsidiary laboratory of the department, which was then under the General Hospital. The hospital was later renamed Braithwaite Hospital. His colleagues in Port Harcourt were D. A. Pratt, Henry Durosimi Eti, and Messrs. Bassey, Okun, and Green. There was also a Mr. Macaulay, who died in 1941, shortly after they had made an acquaintance. Other friends later became governors, assemblymen, members of the judiciary, and leading civil servants. They included justices Gaston Martins and Barclay Purple.

Avocationally, Papa was a member of the All-Purpose Committee of his social club in Port Harcourt of which a Mr. Ajegbo was the secretary. He was also a member of the UNA Church with Bishop Adeniran as the shepherd. It was under Bishop Adeniran's mentorship that Papa, at the tender age of twenty, began testifying, preaching, and raising funds for the laying of the foundation stone that led to the erection of St. Paul's UNA Church on Aggrey Road in Port Harcourt.

In 1944, Sir Akinbomi Savage returned to western Nigeria to establish a laboratory of the Chemistry Department of the Ministry of Water Works at Eleyele Village, Ibadan, the capital of the present Oyo State. The stated purpose of the laboratory was to check the bacteriological content of the water in the village. In the same year, the Nigerian army occupied a portion of Eleyele Village; but soon afterward, it became the site of the University of Ibadan. As a consequence of its salubriousness, the village became a picnic location for many residents of the area. Papa's socialite friends from those days at the Yaba Club in Ibadan included Akin Deko and Messrs. Bateye and Aripo. Relaxation often took the form of listening to radio programs featuring music requests and editorials.

Papa bought his first motorcycle in 1946 and, at the end of 1948, a used automobile that proved to be rather expensive to maintain. It was at this time that he met and married Ernestina Modupe Macaulay, then a spinster from the Olowogbowo area of Lagos Island. They remained married until his sudden demise in 2007. Mrs. Ernestina Modupe Savage is a descendant of Herbert Macaulay, the acknowledged Father of Nigerian Nationalism.

In June 1950, Sir Akinbomi Savage proceeded abroad to the United Kingdom in search of the Golden Fleece. He docked at Liverpool and then travelled to

London, courtesy of the English government. Within two days of his arrival in London, he was whisked off to Barnsley, Yorkshire. The British council had arranged for him to live in a miner's hostel. He was introduced to the colliery staff at the main office and began work in the coal mines in order to support himself. As one can imagine, life in the coal mines of Yorkshire was virtually diabolical for a former laboratory technician. He was joined in 1951 by his wife, Mrs. Ernestina Modupe Savage and, later, by the author. For seven years, he rented some rooms at 17 Longman Road in Barnsley from a caring landlady, Mrs. Dorothy Watson, before being able to purchase his own house at 43 Rock Street, Barnsley. His dearest friends in Barnsley were Mr. and Mrs. Fred Holland with whose children—Judy, Sandra, and Martin—the author was raised. Papa enrolled at the University of Sheffield where he studied and qualified as a colliery engineer. Upon graduation, he worked for the British National Coal Board, Barnsley, in the northeast county of Yorkshire, England, where he rose to be a colliery manager.

Whilst in Barnsley, the Savage family attended St. George's Church where the author was a chorister. In those days, Reverend Meanley was the shepherd of the church. The author also attended the church's mission and secondary schools as well as being very active in its Boy Scout troop. Vacations were spent in resorts such as Blackpool, Great Yarmouth, and Brighton, as well as in London, during bank holidays. On one occasion, Papa visited France to study the ironstone mines and took a day trip to Luxemburg. Sir Akinbomi Savage spent ten and a half years in the United Kingdom.

Papa returned to Nigeria in December 1960, having received an appointment to join the Nigerian Coal Corporation while still in England. He served mainly in the then eastern region of Nigeria. He worked diligently and meritoriously for the Nigerian Coal Corporation, even during the inception of the civil war, rising to the level of grade 14.

There is a huge difference between working in the coal mines of Barnsley and those of Enugu. The coal fields of Yorkshire are well developed and concealed; hence, mining is now at great depths. Mining in Enugu is still at the surface level. There is less fear of dangerous conditions involved in conducting surface mining than there is in going down in the pits of a concealed coalfield. For a while, Papa even worked in Odaka, Nigeria; and mining there was opencast mining, involving even less depth in finding coal.

Work in Enugu was interrupted in 1967 by the Biafra War, which lasted from July 6, 1967, until January 15, 1970. All non-Eastern Nigerians were obliged to leave the east, and Papa was not an exception. His best friend in the Nigerian Coal Corporation, Mr. Agu, warned of the impending danger; and the author's family returned to Lagos. For several months following his return to Lagos, Sir Akinbomi communicated with Enugu in a vain attempt to continue mining in the east.

As it became obvious that coal was no longer reaching Lagos and parts of the north, a new company was formed with the intention of finding new coalfields. This company was the New Nigerian Development Corporation (NNDC). Papa was invited to join the company, and he began excavating in the midwest, eventually settling in a village named Ankpa in Kwara State, from which mining of a sort could be forged. The mining was very rudimentary and required a great deal of excavation and digging trial wells to determine at what depth coal might be found. Life was very difficult in Ankpa in those days because the town barely existed as it was provincial territory. Even the basics of life were difficult to come by. There were two primary schools, a Catholic church, a Protestant church, and a few government buildings. Papa helped to sustain the Protestant church, even arranging for a visit from the bishop of the diocese. Papa became the bishop's nominee for the area. Ankpa was jostled about between various states as it became a viable center of industrialization. At differing times, the states of Kwara, Benue-Plateau, and Kogi all vied for its inclusion in their state; such were the burgeoning mineral rewards of the area. Sir Akinbomi was the manager of the Ankpa Office for about eight years. He later returned to Enugu for about six years before eventually retiring from the industry in 1982.

In appreciation of his services to the nation, the Federal Government of Nigeria recognized his contributions to Nigeria's industrialization and awarded him the national honor of the Member of the Order of the Niger (MON) in 1983.

Sir Akinbomi Savage practiced the tenets of the maxim "*Do unto others as you expect to be done unto you.*" He joined the Young Men's Auxiliary Association of St. Paul's Church, Breadfruit, in 1990 and remained passionate about the society, cheerfully looking forward to its monthly meetings. We are made to understand that he was quite vociferous at the last meeting of the association that he attended in March 2007.

Papa was very conscious not to inconvenience other people. He was a gentleman, selfless, humble, reserved, and an Anglophile. Though he had failing health in his latter days, his wish was to pass away peacefully, which the good Lord granted him.

He is survived by his wife, children, grandchildren, nephews, nieces, and in-laws.

May his gentle soul rest in perfect peace and eternal glory! AMEN.

Savage, Sir Josiah Akinbomi. Personal Communication. July 25, 2006.

==

Hon. Justice William Akibo Savage, LLD, OFR.

(March 7, 1916-November 27, 2001)

Jurist

Hon. Justice Akibo Savage was born on March 7, 1916, at Calabar, Cross River State, Nigeria, to the well-known and illustrious Savage family of Abeokuta and Olowogbowo, Lagos.

His parents were the Late William Akilade Kodeleyiri Savage, barrister at law of the Middle Temple, London, and the late Gladys Ibidunni Savage of the Aromire family of Isale Eko, Lagos.

For a brief period, Justice Savage received his elementary school education at Onisha Central School, after which his parents returned to Lagos in 1928. He continued his education at the Church Missionary Society Grammar School, Broad Street, Lagos, from 1929 to 1931. He attended King's College (high school) in 1932 and graduated in 1936 after obtaining his Senior Oxford School Certificate (high school diploma). Some of his high school classmates were the late Dr. Vanderpauye, Bassey Ikpeme, Gesinde, Dr. Cookey Gam, and Dr. Irene Thomas.

The transcript of Justice Savage's Oxford examination (junior high school certificate) bears witness to his tactile prowess as he received special commendation for his artwork. During the period from 1932 to 1936, young Akibo Savage won the King's College Art Prize annually. He also had the distinction of being a King's College house prefect.

After leaving King's College, Justice Savage taught briefly at Eko Boys High School and later worked at the Royal Exchange Assurance Company for many years before proceeding to the United Kingdom to study law. He was called to the English Bar at the Middle Temple, Inns of Court, London, in 1957 after which he returned to Nigeria in 1959 and practiced law.

The late Honorable Justice Akibo Savage married the then Miss Pamela Evelyn Moore on July 20, 1944. They are blessed with two beautiful daughters—Dr. (Mrs.) Victoria Yewande Olusola and Mrs. Effrida Omotara Abayomi, BL, LLM—and six grandchildren.

Hon. Justice Akibo Savage was appointed a magistrate, grade 1, on October 17, 1960. The chief justice of Nigeria at the time, the Honorable Mr. Nageon de Lestang, highly commended his legal expertise and appointed him as a senior magistrate on January 21, 1966. Such was Justice Savage's reputation for fairness and thoroughness that by 1967, the late Honorable Justice J. I. Conrad Taylor, chief judge of Lagos State, promoted him to become the deputy chief registrar of the Lagos State High Court.

On May 20, 1968, the talents of the late Justice Akibo Savage were further recognized by the then chief justice of Nigeria, the late Sir Adetokunboh Ademola. The chief justice elevated Attorney Savage to serve as the chief registrar of the Supreme Court of Nigeria.

In August 1972, the late Justice Akibo Savage was appointed as the secretary to the All Judges Conference, which dedicated itself to considering ways and means of improving the administration of justice in Nigeria. On October 1, 1972, the late Honorable Justice Akibo Savage was further decorated when he was appointed to the bench as a judge of the High Court of Lagos State.

In 1978, he served the Lagos State government as the chairman of inquiry into the dispute between the Teaching Service Commission and the Nigerian Union of Teachers, Lagos State branch. His adjudication report was accepted and implemented. In 1979, he was appointed a member of the Election Petition Tribunal for Lagos.

Justice William Akibo Savage retired on March 7, 1983, upon attaining the statutory age of sixty-five. He was the first judge of Lagos State to so retire, having reached retirement age without scandal or recrimination. He was also the first judge to be honored by a valedictorian session of the High Court of Lagos State. In July 1983, he was appointed to the prestigious position of group legal director of the Leventis Group of Companies. On October 1, 1983, a transcendent honor was bestowed on him when he was knighted by the Federal Government of Nigeria with the national award as an Officer of the Federal Republic of Nigeria (OFR).

In February 1984, Hon. Justice Akibo Savage received the approbation of his peers when he was decorated with the position of pro-chancellor and chairman of the governing council of Lagos State University (LASU). He held this position for three years. Furthermore, on August 9, 1985, Justice Savage was appointed as the chairman of the Committee on Remuneration and Classification of Obas and Chiefs of Lagos State.

In familial matters, Justice Savage was the head of the Savage family (*olori-ebi*) for ten years until his death on November 27, 2001. He succeeded Percy Savage, former principal of King's College, Lagos, as the olori-ebi. Transcendentally, he was a member of the Young Men's Auxiliary Association of St. Paul's Church, Breadfruit. Lagos. He was honored on the sixtieth anniversary celebration of the association when he was designated as the life president of the association and chairman of its constitution review panel. In social affairs, Justice Savage was a member of the vanguard Metropolitan Club, which held its meeting at Kofo Abayomi Street on Victoria Island, Lagos. In February 1998, Justice Savage was awarded the honorary degree, *honoris causa*, of Doctor of Laws, LLD, by Lagos State University.

Hon. Justice William Akibo Savage's hobbies included art, painting, and music. He loved and played all kinds of music, but particularly classical music and jazz. In his younger days, he was the pianist of the Rhythm Brothers, a highly popular and hip dance band.

The author last saw Justice Savage on May 20, 2001, in Bethesda, Maryland, USA, at the home of his daughter, Mrs. Omotara Abayomi. It was agreed during that visit that the author would pen an official biography of Justice Savage. Unfortunately, Justice Savage died on November 27, 2001, before he could remit any materials to the author for publication. The task remains unfulfilled.

Savage, Pamela Evelyn. Personal Communication. March 28, 2002.

==

Dr. Akinwande Oluwole Soyinka
(July 13, 1934—)
The First African Nobel Prize Winner in Literature

Wole Soyinka was born in Ijebu Isara and is of Egba descent. His father, Ayo, was a school supervisor; and his mother, Eniola, "a trader." Wole Soyinka is a percipient and prolific critic, novelist, poet, playwright, and recusant political activist.

For over forty-four years, Wole Soyinka has been a perspicacious writer, beginning in 1958 with his florescence in *The Swamp Dwellers* and the publication of *The Lion and the Jewel* in 1959. The 1960s featured *The Trials of Brother Jero* in 1960, ending with *The Road* in 1969. The 1970s produced *Madmen and Specialists* in 1970, *Myth, Literature and the African World* in 1976, and an essay, "Language as Boundary," in 1978. The advent of the 1980s revealed the *Critical Perspective on Wole Soyinka* in 1980 as well as *Ake: The Years of Childhood* in 1989. The very prolific 1990s unveiled *Isara, a Voyage Around "Essays"* in 1991 and, approximately six publications later, *Early Poems* in 1999. Even the twenty-first century has witnessed the fruition of *Conversations with Wole Soyinka*, edited by Biodun Jeyifo, in 2001; *Death and the King's Horsemen* in 2002; and *Samarkand and Other Markets I Have Known* also in 2002.

In 1986, Wole Soyinka was the first African to be awarded the Nobel Prize in Literature. Also in 1986, he was awarded Nigeria's second highest civilian honor, the Commander of the Federal Republic (CFR). Furthermore, Harvard University, in the United States of America, arguably the premier university in the world, recognized his literary preeminence with a doctorate, *honoris causa*, in 1993.

On a personal note, the author first met Wole Soyinka when Wole was a senior lecturer in the English Department at the University of Lagos, Nigeria. As our undergraduate professor in English literature, my peers and I asked him why he had returned to Nigeria without earning his doctorate degree from Leeds University in England. Completing a doctorate degree was our avowed aim in academia. With unabashed candor, Professor Soyinka's laconic retort was, "I plan to begin my doctoral studies in the near future"—an epexegesis was not needed for this audience. We were all appropriately impressed since we had witnessed his erudition firsthand. Professor Soyinka was not bragging by this comment; he merely wanted to reiterate his confidence that he was sufficiently well-schooled to begin his academic career without formally completing a Ph.D. degree at that time. He earned his doctorate in 1973. Of course, his profundity was further averred later when he was awarded the Nobel Prize in Literature in 1986.

Gibbs, James. *Wole Soyinka.* Westport, Connecticut: Greenwood Press, 1988.

Jones, Eldred Durosimi. *The Writings of Wole Soyinka.* London: Heinemann, 1983.

Maja-Pearce, Adewale, ed. *Wole Soyinka: An Appraisal.* Oxford: Heinemann, 1994.

===

Madam Tinubu

(1805-1887)

First Iyalode of Egbaland, Abolitionist

Madam Tinubu was born in Ojokodo in the Gbagura section of Abeokuta. She survived the death of her first husband and two sons by immersing herself in a lucrative business in salt, tobacco, and slaves, trading between Abeokuta and Badagry. Her second husband was an Oba in Lagos, and it was during this period of time, as the Olori, that she acquired her political prowess. Her third husband was a confidant in the Oba's court, and she also became politically influential in the palace. When King Akitoye of Lagos was deposed in 1846, he first exiled in Abeokuta, his maternal home, but transplanted to Badagry at the suggestion of Madam Tinubu. When Oba Akitoye was reinstalled as the king of Lagos in 1851, Madam Tinubu decided to relocate to Lagos where she became a state adviser. King Akitoye died in 1853 and was succeeded by his son King Dosumu. Almost inevitably, Madam Tinubu's influence expanded, leading to accusations that the king was weak. Her burgeoning influence in Lagos earned her the ire of British officials and merchants, who engineered King Dosumu to excommunicate her.

In 1857, she took up residence in Abeokuta, where she once more effloresced as a merchant and a politician. To cite an example of her activities, Madam Tinubu's initial political machinations as a kingmaker were frustrated in 1862. However, her brokering came to fruition in 1879 when her nominee, Oyekan, became the third Alake of Abeokuta. Oba Oyekan merely succeeded Alake Ademola I rather than Alake Okukenu. Subsequently, Madam Tinubu benefited accordingly during Alake Oyekan's truncated reign. Furthermore, Madam Tinubu was pivotally instrumental in the successful repulsion of the Dahomey invasion of Abeokuta in 1864 by serving as a quartermaster and encouraging the troops. Reportedly, in order to ensure victory, she actually fought along with the hoplitic troops (Mba: 9). Consequently, she was rewarded for these accomplishments by being recognized as the first Iyalode of Egbaland—the chief of women in Abeokuta. Madam Tinubu's myriad successes illustrate the acceptance and influence of women in the unwritten monarchical constitution of Abeokuta.

Madam Tinubu has been likened to Queen Boadicea, the legendary British Queen of Iceni, who died in AD 62; to Queen Elizabeth I of England (1558-1603); and even to Joan of Arc (1412-1431), because she successfully financed the defense of Abeokuta and Lagos against their enemies. The construction of Tinubu Square in the very heart of downtown Lagos established Madam Tinubu as a national heroine. The city of Abeokuta also honored her with the erection of a monument at Ita Iyalode in Owu. Madam Tinubu died on December 3, 1887, and is buried in her natal city of Ojokodo in the Gbagura section of Abeokuta.

———

Biobaku, Saburi O. "Madam Tinubu." *Eminent Nigerians of the Ninteenth Century.* London: Oxford University Press, 1966.

==

Frederick Rotimi Williams

(December 1920—)

Barrister at Law

Frederick Rotimi Williams was born on December 16, 1920. His education included attending the CMS Grammar School, Lagos, and Cambridge University, England. He was a member of the Western Region (of Nigeria) Committee on new regional legislation, which visited London, Australia, and the United States of America in 1954. Barrister Williams was for many years a state minister in the then Western Region of Nigeria. Attorney Rotimi Williams is now in private law practice and is married with children.

==

REFERENCES

BOOKS

Abimbola, 'Wande and Barry Hallen. "Secrecy and Objectivity in the Methodology and Literature of Ifa Divination," *Secrecy: African Art that Conceals and Reveals.* P. Nooter, ed. New York: The Museum for African Art, and Munich: Prestel, 1978.

Abimbola, 'Wande. *Ifa: An Exposition of Ifa Literary Corpus.* New York: Athelia Henrietta Press, 1997.

Achebe, Chinua. *Things Fall Apart.* Oxford: Heinemann Educational Publishers, 1958.

————. *Arrow of God,* New York: Anchor Books, 1969.

Adebo, Chief Simeon O. *Our Unforgettable Years.* Lagos: Macmillan Nigeria Publishers, 1984.

Adedeji, Adebayo, ed. *An Introduction to Western Nigeria: Its People, Culture and System of Government.* London: Hutchinson, 1968.

Adekanbi, Sola. *The Yoruba Way: A Handbook of Yoruba Customs.* Lagos: the author, 1955.

Ademoyega, Wale. *The Federation of Nigeria.* London: G. G. Harrap, 1962.

Adenikan, S. K. *Abeokuta Heroes*. Ibadan: The Lisabi Press.

Aderibigbe, A. A. B. "People of Southern Nigeria." *A Thousand Years of West African History*. J. F. Ajayi and Ian Espie, eds. New York: Humanities Press, 1972.

Adewale, S. A. *The Religion of the Yoruba: A Phenomenological Analysis*. Ibadan, Nigeria: Department of Religious Studies, University of Ibadan, 1988.

Afigbo, A. E., et al. *The Making of Modern Africa*. 2 vols. Academic Press; London: Frank Cass, 1986.

Ajayi, J. F. Ade. *Christian Missions in Nigeria: 1841-1891*. London: Longmans, 1965.

————, "The Continuity of African Institutions under Colonialism." *Emerging Themes of African History*, pp. 190-199. T Ranger, ed. Nairobi: East African Publishing House, 1968.

————, and Robert Smith, eds. *Yoruba Warfare in the Nineteenth Century*. Ibadan: University of Ibadan, 1971.

————, and Michael Crowder, eds. *History of West Africa*. New York: Columbia University Press, 1972.

————, and S. Adebanji Akintoye "Yorubaland in the nineteenth century." *Groundwork of Nigerian history*. Ibadan: Heinemann Educational Books, 1980: pp. 280-302.

Ajisafe, Ajayi Kolawole. *History of Abeokuta*. Lagos: Kash & Klare Bookshop, 1948.

Akinjogbin, I. A. *Dahomey and Its Neighbours, 1708-1818*. Cambridge: Cambridge University Press, 1967.

————. "Origin and History of the Yoruba." *An Introduction to Western Nigeria: Its People, Culture and System of Government*. Adebayo Adedeji, ed. London: Hutchinson, 1968.

Akintoye, S. Adebanji. *Revolution and Power Politics in Yorubaland, 1840-93: Ibadan Expansion and the Rise of Ekitiparapo.* New York: Humanities Press, 1971.

———. *Emergent African States: Topics in twentieth century African history.* London: Longman, 1976.

———. *A History of the Yoruba People.* Amalion Publishing, 2010.

Akinyele, I. B. *Iwe Itan Ibadan.* Lagos: Alebiosu Printing Press, 1946.

Alderfer, Harold F. *Local Government in Developing Countries.* New York: McGraw-Hill, 1964.

Apthorpe, Raymond, ed. *From Tribal Rule to Modern Government.* Lusaka: Rhodes-Livinston Institute, 1960.

Ayandele. E. A. *The Educated Elite in the Nigerian Society.* Ibadan: Ibadan University Press, 1974.

Awolalu, J. Omosade. *Yoruba Beliefs and Sacrificial Rites.* New York: Athelia Henrietta Press, 1966.

Awolowo, Obafemi. *Path to Nigerian Freedom.* London: Faber & Faber, 1947.

———. *Thoughts on the Nigerian Constitution.* Ibadan: Oxford University Press, 1966.

Bascom, William. *The Yoruba of South Western Nigeria.* New York: Holt, Rinehart & Winston Inc., 1969.

Biobaku, Saburi O. *The Lugard Lectures.* Lagos: Federal Information Service, 1955.

———. *The Egba and Their Neighbours, 1842-1872.* London: Oxford University Press, 1957.

———. *The Origin of the Yoruba.* Lagos: Federal Ministry of Information, 1960.

———. "Madam Tinubu." *Eminent Nigerians of the Nineteenth Century*. London: Oxford University Press, 1966.

———. ed. *Sources of Yoruba History*. Oxford: Clarendon Press, 1973.

———. *When We Were Young. Ibadan*: University Press PLC, 1992.

———. *A Window on Nigeria*. Lagos: Nelson Publishers, 1994.

Bottomore, T. B. *Elites and Society*. New York: Basic Books, 1965.

Burns, Sir Alan. *History of Nigeria*. London: George Allen & Unwin, 1969.

Burton, Richard Francis. *Abeokuta and the Cameroons Mountains: An exploration*. London: Tinsley Brothers, 1863.

Byfield, Judith A. *The Bluest Hands: A Social and Economic History of Women Dyers in Abeokuta (Nigeria), 1890-1940*. Portsmouth, New Hampshire: Heinemann, 2000.

Coleman, James S. *Nigeria: Background to Nationalism*. Berkeley: University of California Press, 1965.

Crowder, Michael. *A Short History of Nigeria*. London: Faber & Faber, 1962.

———. *West Africa Under Colonial Rule*. Evanson, Ill.: Northwestern University Press, 1968.

———. and Obaro Ikime, *West African Chiefs—Their Changing Status Under Colonial Rule and Independence*. New York: Africana Publishing Corp, 1970.

Curtin, Philip D. *Africa Remembered: Narratives by West Africans from the Era of the Slave Trade*. Madison, Milwaukee: The University of Wisconsin Press, 1967.

Curtin, Philip D. *Africa and the West: Intellectual Responses to European Culture*. Madison: University of Wisconsin Press, 1972.

Cutter, Charles H. *Africa 2002.* Baltimore: United Book Press, 2002.

Duiker, William J. *Twentieth-Century World History.* Belmont, CA: West/ Wadsworth, 1999.

Egharevba, J. U. *A Short History of Benin.* Ibadan: Ibadan University Press, 1968.

Falola, Toyin. *The History of Nigeria.* Westport, Connecticut: Greenwood Press, 1999.

———. *Culture and Customs of Nigeria.* Westport, Connecticut: Greenwood Press, 2001.

Findley, Carter Vaughn, and John Alexander Murray Rothney. *Twentieth-Century World.* 5th ed. Boston, Massachusetts: Houghton Mifflin Company, 2002.

Folarin, A. *Egba History: Life Review 1829-1930.* Chicago: University of Chicago Press, 1969.

Forde, Cyril Daryll. *The Yoruba-Speaking Peoples of Southwestern Nigeria.* London: International African Institute, 1951.

———. and P. M. Kaberry, eds. *West African Kingdoms in the Nineteenth Century.* London: Oxford University Press for International African Institute, 1967.

Gailey, Harry A. *Lugard and the Abeokuta Uprising: The Demise of Egba Independence.* Bodmin, Cornwall: Frank Cass, 1982.

Geary, Sir William N. M. *Nigeria Under British Rule.* New York: Barnes & Noble, 1965.

George, Chief John Akinwunmi. *Industrial and Economic Development in Nigeria: Selected Issues.* Lagos: Malthouse Press, 2002.

Goff, Richard et. al. *The Twentieth Century: A Brief Global History.* 5th ed. Boston, Massachusetts: McGraw-Hill, 1998.

Gwam, Lloyd C. *Great Nigerians*. Lagos: A *Daily Times* Publication, 1967.

Hailey, Lord W. M. *Native Administration in the British African Territories: Parts III and IV*. London: H. M. Stationary Office, 1954.

———. *African Survey*. London: Oxford University Press, 1957.

———. *Native Administration and African Political Development*. London: Oxford University Press, 1957.

Harris, Joseph E. *Global Dimensions of the African Diaspora*. 2nd ed. Washington, D.C.: Howard University Press, 1993.

Idowu, E. B. *Olodumare: God in Yoruba Belief*. London: Longmans, 1962.

Johnson, Rev. S. *The History of the Yorubas*. London: Lowe & Brydone, 1921.

Johnson-Odim, Cheryl, and Nina Emma Mba. *For Women and the Nation*: *Fumilayo Ransome-Kuti of Nigeria*. Urbana and Chicago: University of Illinois Press, 1997.

Johnson-Odim, Cheryl, and Margaret Strobel. "Funmilayo Ransome-Kuti and the Struggles for Nigerian Independence and Women's Equality." *Expanding the Bounds of Women's History: Essays on Women in the Third World*. Bloomington and Indianapolis: Indiana University Press, 1992.

Karunwi, Omodele. *A Woman Industrialist: A Biography of Chief (Mrs.) Bisoye Tejuoso. Yeye-Oba, Oke-Ona Egba. 3rd Iyalode of Egbaland*. Lagos: Cowlad Enterprises, Nigeria, 1991.

Keay, E. A., and S. S. Richardson. *The Native and Customary Courts of Nigeria*. Lagos: African Universities Press, 1966.

Kilson, Martin. *Political Change in a West African State: A Study of the Modernization Process in Sierra Leone*. New York: Atheneum, 1969.

————. "Emergent Elites in Black Africa." *Colonialism in Africa, 1870-1960.* Vol. 2: *The History and Politics of Colonialism, 1914-1960.* London: Cambridge University Press, 1970.

Kirk-Green, A. H. M. *The Principles of Native Administration in Nigeria: Selected Documents, 1900-1947.* London: Oxford University Press, 1965.

Kopytoff, Jean H. *A Preface to Modern Nigeria.* Milwaukee, Wis.: University of Wisconsin Press, 1965.

Kuti, Hon. Justice Ademola. *Ten Years On. A Decade of Royal Selfless Service: Salute to Kabiyesi Alaiyeluwa Oba Dr. Adedapo Adewale Tejuoso.* Ibadan: Intec Printers, 1999.

Losi, J. B. O. *History of Abeokuta.* Lagos: CMS Bookshop, 1930.

————. *History of Lagos.* Lagos: African Educational Press, 1967.

Lloyd, P. C. *The New Elites of Tropical Africa.* London: Oxford University Press, 1966.

————, A. L. Mabogunje, and Bolanle Awe, eds. *The City of Ibadan.* London: Cambridge University Press, 1967.

————. *The Political Development of Yoruba Kingdoms in the Eighteenth and Nineteenth Centuries.* London: Royal Anthropological Institute, 1971.

————. "Political and Social Structure." *Sources of Yoruba History.* S. O. Biobaku, ed. Oxford: Clarendon Press, 1973.

Lugard, Lord Frederick. *The Dual Mandate in British Tropical Africa, 1921.* 5th ed. Hamden, Conn.: Archon Books, 1965.

Mabogunje, A. L. *Urbanization in Nigeria.* London: University of London Press, 1968.

————, and J. D. Omer-Cooper. *Owu in Yoruba History.* Ibadan: Ibadan University Press, 1971.

Mba, Nina Emma. *Nigerian Women Mobilized: Women's Political Activity in Southern Nigeria, 1900-1965*. Berkeley: University of California, Institute of International Studies, 1982.

Mertz, Helen Chapin, ed. *Nigeria: A Country Study*. Washington, D.C.: Federal Research Division of the Library of Congress, 1992.

Mills, C. Wright. *Power Elite*. New York: Oxford University Press, 1957.

Moore, Kofoworola Aina. "The Story of Kofoworola Aina Moore, of the Yoruba Tribe, Nigeria." *Ten Africans*, Margery Perham, ed. London: Faber and Faber, 1936.

Morel, E. D. *Nigeria, Its People and Its Problems*. London: Frank Cass & Co., 1968.

Nixon, Howard L. *The Small Group*. Englewood Cliffs, N. J.: Prentice Hall Inc., 1979.

Obasanjo, General Olusegun. *My Command: An Account of the Nigerian Civil War, 1967-1970*. Ibadan, Nigeria: Heinemann, 1980.

Odunoye, Oladipo, Olalekan Akinpelu, and 'Wale Ope-Agbe. *Oba Oyebade Lipede: A Great Egba Monarch*. Lagos: Opeds Nigeria Limited, 1997.

Ogunshakin, Patrick. *Olumo*. Surulere, Lagos; Toklast Enterprises, 1992.

Ola, Opeyemi. *Local Government in West Africa: An Annotated Bibliography*. Ibadan: Ibadan University Press, 1967.

Olanlokun, Olajire. *The Legend: Sir Ahmadu Bello*. Lagos, Nigeria: Literamed Publications (Nig.) 2001.

———. *The Legend: Obafemi Awolowo*. Lagos, Nigeria: Literamed Publications (Nig.) 2003.

Olusanya, Gabriel O. *Memoirs of a Disillusioned Patriot*. Ibadan, Nigeria: Helicon Press, 2003.

Paulme, Denise, ed. *Women in Tropical Africa*. Translated by H. M. Wright. Berkeley: University of California Press, 1971.

Peel, J. D. Y. *Ijeshas and Nigerians: The Incorporation of a Yoruba Kingdom, 1890s-1970s. New York: Cambridge University Press, 1983.*

————. *Religious Encounters and the Making of the Yoruba*. Bloomington: Indiana University Press, 2000.

Perham, Margery, ed. *Ten Africans*. London: Faber and Faber, 1936.

————. *Lugard: The Years of Authority, 1898-1945*. London: Collins, 1961.

————. *Native Administration in Nigeria*. London: Oxford University Press, 1962.

Reynolds, Edward. *Stand the Storm: A History of the Atlantic Slave Trade*. Chicago: Ivan R. Dee, 1993.

Sklar, Richard L. *Nigerian Political Parties*. Princeton: Princeton University Press, 1963.

Smith, Robert. *Kingdoms of the Yoruba*. London: Methuen Co., 1969.

Smythe, Hugh H., and Mabel M. Smythe. *The New Nigerian Elite*. Stanford, CA: Stanford University Press, 1960.

Soyinka, Wole. *The Lion and the Jewel. London: Oxford University Press, 1959 and 1996.*

————. *The Swamp Dwellers, 1959.*

————. *The Trials of Brother Jero, 1960.*

————. *The Interpreters, London: Trafalgar Square, 1965.*

————. *The Road, 1965.*

————. *A Dance of the Forest, 1966.*

————. *Kongi's Harvest, 1967.*

————. *Idanre and Other Poems,* 1967.

————. *Madmen and Specialists, 1970.*

————. *A Shuttle in the Crypt,* 1972.

————. *Season of Anomy, 1973.*

————. *Collected Plays (including A Dance of the Forest, The Swamp Dwellers, The Strong Breed, The Road, The Bacchae of Euripides), 1973.*

————. *Collected Plays 2, 1975.*

————. *Myth, Literature and the African World,* 1976.

————. *Language as Boundary,* 1978.

————. *Critical Perspective on Wole Soyinka,* 1980.

————. *Ake: The Years of Childhood, 1981.*

————. *The Man Died,* 1988.

————. *Art, Dialogue & Outrage: Essays on Literature and Culture,* 1988.

————. *Mandela's Earth and Other Poems,*1988.

————. *Isara, a Voyage Around "Essays.", 1991.*

————. *The Open Sore of a Continent: A Personal Narrative of the Nigerian Crisis,* 1997.

————. *The Trials of Brother Jero and the Strong Breed,* 1998.

————. *The Burden of Memory, the Muse of Forgiveness,* 1998.

————. *Soyinka,* 1999.

————. *Early Poems,* 1999.

————. *Conversations with Wole Soyinka,* ed. Biodun Jeyifo, 2001.

————. *Death and the King's Horsemen,* 2002.

————. *Samarkand and Other Markets I Have Known, 2002.*

————. *You Must Set Forth at Dawn: A Memoir,* 2006.

Sunderland, Dorothy B. *Enchantment of the World: Nigeria.* Chicago: Children's Press, 1995.

Talbot, P. A. *The People of Southern Nigeria.* London: Oxford University Press, 1926.

Tamuno, Tukano N. *Nigeria and Elective Representation, 1923-47.* London: Heinemann, 1966.

Thomas, Hugh. *The Slave Trade: The Story of the Atlantic Slave Trade, 1440-1870.* New York: Simon & Schuster, 1997.

Utomi, Pat. *To Serve is to Live: Autobiographical reflections on the Nigerian condition.* Ibadan: Spectrum Books, 1999.

Vaughn, Olufemi. *Nigerian Chiefs: Traditional Power in Modern Politics, 1890s-1990s.* Camden House, 1996.

Walter, Rodney. *How Europe Underdeveloped Africa.* Wahington, D.C.: Howard University Press, 1981.

Who's Who in Nigeria: A Biographical Dictionary. Lagos: Daily Times Press: A Daily Times Division Publication, 1971.

Zachernuk. Philip S. *Colonial Subjects: An African Intelligensia and Atlantic Ideas.* Charlottesville: University Press of Virginia, 2000.

JOURNALS

Arnett, E. J. "Native Administration in West Africa, a Comparison of French and British Policy." *African Affairs* 32 (July 1933): 240-51.

Avery, W. L. "Concepts of God in Africa." *Journal of the American Academy of Religion*, vol. 39, no. 3 (1971): 391.

Ballard, J. A. "Administrative Origins of Nigerian Federalism." *African Affairs* 70 (October 1971): 333-48.

Biobaku, S. O. "An Historical Sketch of Egba Traditional Authorities." *Africa* 22 (January 1952): 35-49.

Calloway, Barbara. "Local Politics in Ho and Aba." *Canadian Journal of African Studies* 4 (Winter 1940): 121-44.

Dennett, R. E. "The Ogboni and Other Secret Societies in Nigeria." *African Affairs* 16 (October 1916): 16-29.

Hans, Carol. "The Making of Nigeria's Political Regions." *Journal of Asian and* African *Studies* 3 (July 1968): 271-86.

Igbafe, Phillip A. "The Benin Water-Rate Agitation 1937-1939, an Example of Social Conflict." *Journal of the Historical Society of Nigeria* 4 (December 1968): 355-74.

Lloyd, P. C. "The Development of Political Parties in Western Nigeria." *The American Political Science Review* 49 (September 1955): 705-8.

Magid, Alvin. "British Rule and Indigenous Organization in Nigeria: A Case Study in Normative-Institutional Change." *Journal of African History* 9 (1968): 299-313.

Miller, Robert A. "Elite Formation in Africa." *Journal of Modern African Studies* 12 (1957): 521-42.

Oduwobi, Tunde. "Politics in Colonial Ijebu, 1921-51: The Role and Challenge of the Educated Elite." *Canadian Journal of History*, 00084107, Autumn 2006, Vol. 41, Issue 2

Ola, Opeyemi. "Local Government in West Africa." *Journal of Modern African Studies* 6 (1968): 233-48.

Oyewumi, Oyeronke. "Conceptualizing Gender: The Eurocentric Foundations of Feminist Concepts and the Challenge of African Epistemologies." *Jenda: A Journal of Culture and African Women Studies*: 2, 1, (2002).

Pallinder-Law, Agneta. "Aborted Modernization in West Africa: The Case of Abeokuta." *Journal of African History* 15 (1974): 65-82.

Peel, J. D. Y. "Olaju: A Yoruba Concept of Development." *Journal of Development Studies* 14 (1978): 135-165.

Perham, Margery. "A Re-statement of Indirect Rule." *Africa* 7 (July 1934): 321-34.

Phillips, Earl. "The Egba at Abeokuta: Acculturation and Political Change." *Journal of African History* 10 (1969): 117-31.

Prescott, J. R. V. "The Evolution of Nigeria's Boundaries." *Nigerian Geographical Journal 2* (March 1959): 80-104.

Solanke, Ladipo. "The Ogboni Institution in Yoruba." *Wasu: Journal of the West African Students' Union of Great Britain*, vol.1, December 1926: 28-34.

Sklar, Richard L. "Contradictions in the Nigerian Political System." *Journal of Modern African Studies* 3 (August 1965): 201-13.

Walls, Andrew F. "Samuel Ajayi Crowther (1807-1891): Foremost African Christian of the Nineteenth Century." *International Bulletin of Missionary Research 16, issue 1* (January 1992): 15-21.

"Where Do We Come In?" *The West African Review* 8 (September 1937): 1-15.

INTERNET RESOURCES

Abeokuta
  <http://www.uq.net.au/~zzhsoszy/states/nigeria/abeokuta.html>
  Retrieved August 13, 2003

Biography of Alake Ademola II of Abeokuta—Dr. Akinniyi Savage, author
  <http://www.africaexpert.org/people/profiles/profilesforperson4231.html>
  Retrieved December 3, 2002

  <http://en.wikipedia.org/wiki/User:King_of_Abeokuta>
  Retrieved September 18, 2009

Biography of Alake Adedotun Gbadebo III of Abeokuta
  <http://nm.onlinenigeria.com/templates/?a=4288&z=12.>
  Retrieved September 18, 2009

  <http://www.egbaewa.org/Alake.htm.>
  Retrieved September 18, 2009

  <http://nigeriaworld.com/articles/2007/aug/243.html.>
  Retrieved September 18, 2009

Educational materials on Africa
  <http://www.africaresource.com/index.htm>
  Retrieved August 19, 2003

Egba history
  <http://www.egbayewa.org/kingdoms.htm>
  Retrieved September 18, 2009

History of Sierra Leone
  <http://www.africast.com/country_history.php?strCountry=Sierra%20Leone>
  Retrieved February 26, 2003

JENDA: A Journal of Culture and African Women's Studies
  <http://www.jendajournal.com/jenda/vol2.1/toc2.1htm>
  Retrieved August 19, 2003

Landmarks in nineteenth-century Abeokuta
<*http://abeokuta.freeservers.com/History.HTM*>
Retrieved September 18, 2009

Nigeria: Obasanjo in Ogun State Admits Victory of Late Businessman
Abiola. *BBC Monitoring Africa.* London: November 20, 2005, p. 1.
<*http://proquest.umi.com/pqdweb?did=929114261&sid=1&Fmt=3&clie
ntld=19667&RQT=309&VName=PQD*>
Retrieved July 21, 2006

Notable Egba and Egbado
<*http://www.egbaegbado.org/egba13.htm*>
Retrieved August 13, 2003

Oba Michael Adedotun Aremu Gbadebo III
<*http://www.egbayewa.org/kingdoms.htm.*>
Retrieved September 18, 2009

Osahon, Naiwa. *The Correct History of Edo*
<*http://lw14fd.law14.hotmail.msn.com/cgi-bin/getmsg? curmbox
=F000000001&a=d943508.*>.
Retrieved January 15, 2003

Sir Adetokunbo Ademola: His Finest Hour
<*http://www.thisdayonline.com/archive/2003/021820030218law09.html*>
Retrieved August 13, 2003

The Correct History of Edo
<*http://Iw14fd.law.hotmail.msn.com/cgi-bin.getmsg?curmbox=F0000000
01&a=d943508*>
Retrieved January 15, 2003

Walls, Andrew F. *Samuel Ajayi Crowther (1807-1891): Foremost African
Christian of the Nineteenth Century.*
<*http://www.gospelcom.net/chi/BRICABRF/crowther.shtml*>
Retrieved August 18, 2002

GOVERNMENT PUBLICATIONS

Intelligence Reports from the Colonial Office, Great Britain, File Nos. 26/2669 and 26/39215. National Archives, University of Ibadan. (Mimeographed.)

Miller, E.A. Intelligence Reports from the Colonial Office, Great Britain, File No. 26/34231, Chief Secretary's Office, *Abeokuta Intelligence Report 1938: Recommendations for Reorganization*. National Archives, University of Ibadan. (Mimeographed.)

Nigeria. Federal Office of Statistics. *Annual Abstract of Statistics: Nigeria, 1966*. Lagos: Government Printing Office, 1966.

Nigeria. Ministry of Justice. *Native Courts Ordinance, No. 44*. Lagos: Government Printing Office, 1933.

Nigeria. Western House of Assembly. *Western House of Assembly Debates*, NL/L2. Ibadan: Government Printing Office, 1947.

NEWSPAPERS

"Church Missionary Society." *Church Missionary Intelligencer*, 1853.

Daily Times   May 8, 25, 1939;   April 26, 27, 1948;
May 3, 1940;   May 3, 1948;
February 28, 1941;   June 5, 1948;
June 6, 1941;   July 6, 9, 16, 17, 21, 30, 1948;
July 30, 1942;   August 2, 5, 17, 27, 1948;
June 10, 1943;   October 1, 9, 23, 1948;
February 5, 1945;   December 13, 1948;
June 14, 1945;   January 5, 1949;
August 11, 1945;   July 1, 1949;
September 19, 1945;   February 5, 20, 1950;
October 25, 1945;   July 29, 1950;
July 5, 1946; 1950;   August 5, 1950;
September 2, 12, 26,   December 4, 5, 6, 9, 11,
1947;   12, 1950;
December 12, 15,   February 6, 7, 1951.
1947;
August 13, 1992

Headlines (Lagos, Nigeria), No. 49, April 1977.

The West African Pilot November 29, 1947.

UNPUBLISHED PAPERS

Agiri, B. A. "Development of Local Government in Ogbomosho, 1850-1950." Master's thesis. University of Ibadan, 1966.

Ajayi, W.G. A. "A History of the Yoruba Missions, 1843-1880." Master's thesis. University of Bristol, 1959.

Akintoye, S. A. "The Ekitiparapo and the Kiriji War." Ph.D. dissertation. University of Ibadan, 1966.

Brown, Spencer H. "A History of the People of Lagos, 1852-1886." Ph.D. dissertation. Northwestern University, 1964.

Johnson, Cheryl Jeffries. "Nigerian Women and British Colonialism: The Yoruba Example, with Selected Biographies." Ph.D. dissertation. Northwestern University, Evanston, Illinois, 1978.

Mann, Kristin. "A Social History of the New African Elite in Lagos Colony, 1880-1913."Ph.D. dissertation. Stanford University, 1977.

McClure, Amy M. "Local Governments in English-Speaking East and West Africa." Master's thesis. San Diego State College, 1968.

Savage, Akinniyi. "Relationships between Marital Type and Job Performance of Middle Managers in the Financial Services Industry." Ph.D. dissertation. United States International University, 1991.

APPENDICES

APPENDIX 1

A NOTE ON NEWSPAPERS

Since the Nigerian *Daily Times* has been a very invaluable source of information throughout this study, a word about its availability is perhaps in order here. The author read the *Daily Times* in three different locations. These were the National Library in Lagos, Nigeria; the University of Lagos Library; and the National Archives on the campus of the University of Ibadan, Nigeria. Most of the issues were available on microfilm at the time. Other newspapers such as the *West African Pilot* are also available.

APPENDIX 2

A NOTE ON BRITISH GOVERNMENT POLICY PAPERS

The dispatches of the Chief (sometimes called Central) Secretary's Office, under the code name of CSO papers, provide a valuable primary source for local government studies. These policy papers were reports compiled by administrative officers beginning in 1933 with a view to effecting the reorganization of native authorities, clans, districts, divisions, and provinces in Nigeria. The papers such as Abeokuta 21/33010, volume 2, were usually coded with an agency mark, as in "Abeokuta"; a serial number, "21"; a file number, "33010"; and a volume, if applicable. The author read the papers at the national archives on the campus of the University of Ibadan and at the Ministry of Local Government in Ibadan.

INDEX

A

Abacha, Sani, 152, 203
Aba Riots (1929), 112
Abati-George, Adeboye, 165
Abati-George, Iyabode, 168
Abayomi, Effrida Omotara, 218
Abeokuta, 1–2, 25, 118, 146
  arrival of repatriated slaves, 17, 30,
    33, 116, 143
  Christianity, 29–30
  democratization, xi, xiii, 2, 105,
    116, 119
  demographics, 4, 14–15
  education, 89, 105, 117–18, 146
  establishment, 4, 24, 28, 46, 204
  fiscal policies, 94, 96
  levels of government, 31
    Alake, 19, 26, 57
    new elite. *See* saro
    traditional elite. *See* elite,
      traditional
  national anthem, 25
  political development, 3–4, 17, 26,
    30, 103, 118
    British administration, 28, 31, 34,
      57, 60, 115–16, 144

    independence from British
      government, ix, 3, 30–33, 51,
      118, 145
    indirect-rule system, 33, 58, 116,
      119
    shaping factors in, 3–4, 17, 115
  political structures
    Egba Central Council. *See* Egba
      Central Council
    Egba National Council. *See* Egba
      National Council
    Egba United Board of
      Management. *See* Egba United
      Board of Management
    Egba United Government. *See*
      Egba United Government
  power struggles, 92, 96–102,
    117–18
  treaty with Lagos, 13
  women, 3, 117
Abeokuta Ladies' Club. *See* Abeokuta
  Women's Union
Abeokuta Women's Union, 92–96,
  100–101, 105
Abiola, Moshood Kashimawo O., 2,
  72, 147, 151–52
abolitionism, 28

Abraka clan, 88–89

Adebo, Simeon Olaosebikan, 147, 153

Adefolu, Oladunjaye, 59, 160

Adegbenro, Alhaji Dauda Soroye, 154

Ademola, Adetokunbo Adegboyega, 147, 156, 164, 219

Ademola, Ladapo Samuel, II. *See* Ademola II (Alake)

Ademola I (Alake), 44, 48, 53, 59, 67, 98–99, 144, 160, 223

Ademola II (Alake), 44, 58–59, 105, 145, 160
  abdication, xii, 92, 94, 97–98, 100, 105, 117
  accession to Alakeship, 60, 161
  exile, 98, 163
  personal background, 59–60, 159, 161, 164
  reinstatement, 102, 163
  as sole native authority of Abeokuta, 96, 160–61

Aderemi, Adesoji, II, 104, 154

Adesina (son of Sarah Ibikotan), 29, 45, 189

Adesola, Abigail (née Akintola), 205

Ado-Ekiti, 88

Adubi riots (1918), 60, 161

Afala, Hannah, 29

Afonja (generalissimo of the Old Oyo Empire), 54

African Association, 27

AG. *See* Action Group

Agura (king of Gbagura), 21–22

Ajalake (first prominent chief of the Egba), 22

Ake Province, 22, 29, 49, 61, 97, 115

Akinfosile, Olu, 165

Akin-Olugbade, Bolu, 146, 166, 168, 174

Akin-Olugbade, Gladys Ibijoke Iyabode, 165, 167

Akin-Olugbade, Ohu Babatunde, 103, 166–71, 173–74

Akin-Olugbade, Olusunmade Babajimi Aremu, 26, 166, 168, 173–74, 176

Akin-Olugbade, Segun, 166, 168

Akinsanya, Samuel, 212

Akintola, Samuel Ladoke, 103, 154, 166, 169–70

Akiolu, Rilwa, I, xii

Akitoye I (Oba of Lagos), 28, 30, 141–42, 222–23

Alafin, 13, 21, 27

Alake. *See individual Alakes*

Alakiya, Tegumade Assumpcao, 164

Amaro, 17, 30–31, 143

American Baptist Mission, 29

Anikulapo-Kuti, Fela, 177, 179–80, 210

Apomu, 23

Are-Ona-Kakanfo, 21, 146, 171

Awole (Alafin), 23

Awolowo, Obafemi, 7, 103, 111, 232

Azikiwe, Nnamdi, 112, 170, 205

B

Bashorun. *See individual Bashorun*

Benin. *See* Bight of Benin

Benue River, 27, 216

Bight of Benin, 28, 46, 89, 229, 236

Biobaku, Saburi Oladeni, 19, 21–22, 53, 182–83, 196, 199

Blair, J. H., 100

Bolawa, Tolutope A., 166, 168, 174

Bourdillon, Bernard, 87, 109

Bremah, J. K., 178, 180

British, 4, 116
  in Abeokuta, xii, 34, 57, 115, 144
  administration in Lagos, 29
  advent to Nigeria, xii, 17, 27–28, 33
  repatriation movement, xii, 30

C

Cameron, Donald, 86
chief. *See individual chiefs*
Christianity, 27–28, 34, 37–38, 116
Christian Missionary Society. *See* Church Missionary Society of England
Church Missionary Society of England (CMS), 29, 56, 185, 213, 231
civil war. *See individual civil wars*
Clifford, Hugh, 60, 161
CMS. *See* Church Missionary Society of England
Conference of the Chiefs of the Western Provinces, 91, 105, 162
Conference of the Emirs of the Northern Provinces, 90, 162
Conference of Yoruba Chiefs, 91, 162
Conservation Society. *See* Majeobaje Society
Constitution of the Federal Republic of Nigeria, xi
Creole, 185
Crowther, Samuel Ajayi, 9, 28, 30, 147, 184–86, 200, 237, 239

D

Dahomey, 11, 26, 29, 48, 115, 223, 226
Daily Service, 96

Daily Times, 96
Daniel, Otunba Gbenga (Governor), 82
defensive modernizers, 92
de Lestang, Nageon, 218
Delta State, 3
Discours sur l'origine et les fondements de l'inegalite (Rousseau), 27

E

Ebute-Metta, 21–22, 29
ECC. *See* Egba Central Council
Edo State, 3, 42, 46, 65, 239
Edun, Adegboyega, 49, 56–57, 145
Efutike (wife of Chief Okukenu), 29, 205
Egba, 4, 17, 33, 115
  before 1865, 21
  British impact, 4, 28, 31
  list of firsts, 147
  religion, 27, 116
  settlement in western Nigeria, 46
  war effort, 90
  women, xii, 92, 95–96, 101, 117, 119
Egba Agbeyin. *See* Egba Alake
Egba Agura. *See* Gbagura
Egba Alake, 4, 22
Egba Central Council (ECC), 98
  educational policies, 89
  establishment, 85, 105, 117
  representation of women, 94–95, 99, 101, 105, 117
  role during the abdication of the Alake, 22–25, 100–102, 117, 163
  structure, 86–87, 98, 105, 163
  taxation policies, 89, 94, 113
Egbado, 21, 113, 239

Egbaland, 22, 27

Egba National Council (ENC), 61–62, 86–87

Egba Oke-Ona, 4, 22

Egba Owu, 4

Egba United Board of Management (EUBM), 51–54, 57
  failure, 53–54, 61
  goals, 53
  role of the new elite, 52–53, 62, 116

Egba United Government (EUG), 32, 51, 55–56, 98, 163
  achievements, 56
  failure, 57, 61
  role of the new elite, xii, 52, 55, 62

Egba Young Men's Society, 92

Egba Youth League, 92–93, 98, 105, 162

Egbe Atunluse, 92–93, 100–101, 104, 118, 162

Egbe Omo Oduduwa, 92–93, 98, 105

Ekerin, 103, 171

Ekiti, 3, 88, 91

Ekitiland, 88

Ekitiparapo, 88, 227, 242

Ekiti United Government, 88

Elias, Taslim, 147, 187

elite, new educated. *See* saro

elite, traditional, 4, 55, 57, 62, 117–18. *See also* Ogboni; Ologun; Parakoyi

ENC. *See* Egba National Council

EUG. *See* Egba United Government

F

Falae, Olu, 203

Federal Ogun-Oshin River Basin Authority, 15

Fela Ransome-Kuti & Africa 70. *See* Koola Lobitos

Fela Ransome-Kuti and Nigeria 70. *See* Koola Lobitos

Folarin (court president), 89

Fourah Bay College, 185, 211

Fulani, 23, 54, 184

Fulani Jihad, 23, 116

G

Gaha (prime minister of Old Oyo), 21

Gbadebo, Adesina Samuel, II. *See* Gbadebo II (Alake)

Gbadebo, Amoke, 190

Gbadebo, Michael Adedotun Aremu, I. *See* Gbadebo I

Gbadebo, Michael Adedotun Aremu, III. *See* Gbadebo III (Alake)

Gbadebo, Omoba Adesanya Osolake, 190

Gbadebo, Tokunbo, 190

Gbadebo I, 44

Gbadebo II (Alake), 45, 60, 146, 189

Gbadebo III (Alake), 45, 84, 146, 190, 239

Gbagura, 4, 21, 86

George, Elizabeth Ibidapo, 192

George, John Akinwunmi, 192–93

George VI (king of England), 61, 90, 161–62

Ghana, 14, 21, 27, 177, 180

Glover, John Harvey, 29, 53, 141

Gold Coast, 28, 48

Gollmer, C. A., 185

H

Hausa, 3, 41, 185

I

Ibadan, 21, 23, 26, 35–38, 48, 86, 89, 94, 226–29, 231–32, 240, 242, 244–45
  government development, 54–55
  politics, xiii, 13
  population, 14
Ibikotan, Sarah, 29
Ifa Oracle, 18, 25, 44, 191, 225
  gods and godesses, 19
  meaning, 44
    See also Orunmila
  myth of creation, 46
  See also Olorun
Ife, 23, 37, 55, 64, 92, 97, 115
ifole, 29, 47
Igbo, 3, 185
Igbobi College, 189, 213
Ijaye, 21, 23, 26
Ijebu, 13, 21, 23, 94, 237
Ijemo rising, 57
Ile-Ife, 20–22, 35, 37
Ilugun, 23
imperialists, British, 115
indirect rule, 2, 12, 32, 52, 104, 116–17, 119, 142, 237
  in Abeokuta, 31, 93, 97
  and chieftaincy, 91
  end of, 104
  proposal for Ekiti and Ijesha, 88
intelligentsia. *See* Saro
International Court of Justice, 147, 187
Iporo, 91, 191
Islam, 28, 37–39, 116
Isodore, Sandra, 178
iwarefa, 20

J

Jackson, John Payne, 59, 160
Johnson, Esther, 157
Johnson, G. W., 53–55, 59, 67, 160
Jos, 96, 207

K

Kakanfo, 21, 171
Karunwi (Osile of Oke-Ona), 49, 145
King's College, 156, 213, 218–19
Kiriji War, 88, 242
Koola Lobitos, 178–79
Kosoko (Oba of Lagos), 28, 141–42

L

Lagos, 3, 7, 12–13, 22, 35–38, 79, 225, 230–32, 240–42, 244
  British consular period, 28–29
  Egba residents, 55, 93, 101
  liberated slaves at, 30
  political relations with Abeokuta, 55–57, 59, 87, 93, 97
Lagos Weekly Record, 59, 160
Laird, McGregor, 185
Lambo, Adeoye, 147
Lambo, Joseph, 148
Lambo, Sigismund O., 148
Lander, John, 27
Lander, Richard, 27
lineage, xii, 18, 20
Lipede, Michael Mofolorunso Oyebade, 45, 146, 196
Lipede, Oyebade, 149, 191, 196–97, 199–200, 232
Liperu (Abeokuta founder), 24–25, 44, 46

Lisabi (Egba liberator), 21–22, 24–25, 44, 78, 95, 226
local administration, ix, 2
Local Government Law of 1952, xiii, 2, 85, 103–5, 118–19
Lugard, Frederick, 2, 12, 32–33, 38, 48, 57, 63, 116, 142, 227, 229, 233
   Native Administration, 32, 48, 110, 230–31, 233, 236

M

Macaulay, Ernestina Modupe. *See* Savage, Ernestina Modupe
Macaulay, Herbert, 112, 148, 200
Macaulay, T. B., 186
Macpherson Constitution, 104
Majekodunmi (Balogun), 59, 160
Majekodunmi, J. Olutunji, 148
Majekodunmi, Moses Adekoyejo, 155, 201
Majeobaje Society, 93, 96, 102, 104–5, 162, 212
Marshall, H. F., 49
Martins, P. O., 56
McCallum, Henry, 55, 59, 160
Methodist Boys High School, 56, 205, 213
Methodists, 29
Miller (resident), 86
missionaries, 15, 185
   clash with Bishop Crowther, 186
   European, 4, 29, 115
   involvement in politics, 29–31, 53, 57, 115–16
Missionary Society of England, 29, 185
modernists, 54, 57, 103, 164. *See also* traditionalists

modernization, 1–2, 15, 56–57, 92, 116, 230, 237
   arrested, 48
Mohammed, Muritala, 203
Moore, Kofoworola Aina, 148, 159

N

National Council of Nigeria and the Cameroons (NCNC), 95, 104, 112, 169–70, 209, 212
nationalist period, 105
Native Administration (Lugard), 32, 48, 110, 230–31, 233, 236
native administration system, xi, 48, 85, 99, 230–31, 233, 236
   Abeokuta as model of, xi–xii, 2, 58, 85–86, 96–97, 160
   compared with local government, 103
   introduction to western Nigeria, 2, 117
   in Kwale division, 88
native authority, 32, 87, 97–98, 100, 104, 163. *See also* sole native authority
Native Authority Ordinance, 32, 100
Native Courts Ordinance, 32, 110, 240
native court system, 89–90
Native Revenue Ordinance, 32
NCNC. *See* National Council of Nigeria and the Cameroons
neotraditionalists, 92
Niger, River, 27
Niger Coast, 32
Nigeria, x, 5–12, 14, 35, 37–38, 40–48, 64, 76, 79, 117, 195, 210, 225–33, 236–41, 244–45

British arrival, 27, 33
creation, 30, 32, 145
independence, 170
introduction of regional
    government, 104, 112
political divisions, 33
under indirect rule, 32–33
Nigerian Civil War, 203–4, 232
Nigerian Institute of International
    Affairs, 158, 207–8
Nigerian Union of Teachers (NUT),
    212, 219
Nigerian Women's Union, 92
Nigerian Youth Movement (NYM),
    112, 169, 212
Northern People's Congress (NPC),
    169–70

O

Oba. *See names of individual Obas*
Obadimu, Olufemi, 191
Obasanjo, Olusegun, 2, 10, 148,
    202–3
Odimayo, A. Oladele, 195
odu, 18
Oduduwa (mythical figure), 20–22
Odunjo, J. F., 190
Odutola, T. A., 103
Ogboni, 20, 31, 45, 92, 115, 117,
    236–37
    and Alake's ouster, 96–99, 105, 162
    inner council, 61–62, 86
    Reformed Ogboni Fraternity, 158
Ogun River, 10, 15, 24, 168
Ogun State, 4, 10, 12, 36–37, 239
Ogun State Polytechnic, 15
Oil Rivers. *See* Niger Coast
Oke-Ona Province, 23

Okikulu, Oba, 204
Oko Adagba. *See* Abeokuta
Okodi (principal), 166
Okukenu (first Alake of Abeokuta),
    26, 29, 49, 144, 204
Olafioye, Peter, 165
Olakunrin, Toyin, 148
Old Oyo civil war (1754-1774), 21
oligarchy, 31, 116
Olodumare, 18, 38, 43, 230
Ologun, 4, 20, 26, 31, 55–56
Olori, 55, 83, 197, 219, 222
Olorogun. *See* Ologun
Olorun (God of the Yoruba), 18–19,
    43
Olowu, 23, 26, 49, 166, 172, 191,
    213
Olumo Rock, 4, 10, 15, 24–25, 47,
    71, 80–83, 232
Olusanya, Gabriel Olakunle, 205
Olusanya, Joseph Oluwole, 205
Olusola, Victoria Yewande, 218
Oluwaji (Alake), 44, 99, 144
Ondo, 3, 194
Oni, 13, 23, 96, 104, 154, 187, 207
Onikoyi, 23
Oranmiyan (son of Oduduwa), 21
Ordinance No. 44 of 1933, 90
orisas, 18, 36
Orunmila, 44
Oshogbo, 14, 85, 98, 117, 163
Osile, 22, 49, 59, 160
Osun, 3, 21
Owu, 23–26, 97, 115
Owu African Church School, 89
Owu war (1821-1828), 23–24, 54
Oyekan, Adeyinka Akinola
    II, xii, 99, 223
    II. *See* Oyekan II (Oba)

Oyekan I (Alake), 44, 55, 67, 99, 144, 223

Oyekan II (Oba), xii

Oyewumi, Oyeronke, 18, 43

Oyo (town), 3, 15, 55, 97, 115, 143, 152, 184, 214

  Old Oyo, 21, 23, 26

Oyo Empire, 21–23, 26, 143

P

Palmerston, Viscount (Henry John Temple), 28, 142

Parakoyi, 4, 20, 26, 31, 52, 93

Park, Mungo, 27

Pawu (first olowu of Abeokuta), 49, 144

political officers, 2, 4, 86, 88

poll tax, 94–95

progressive unions, 92–93

provinces in Nigeria, 2, 86, 245

R

Ransome-Kuti, Beko, 210

Ransome-Kuti, Fela. *See* Anikulapo-Kuti, Fela

Ransome-Kuti, Israel Oludotun, 93, 162, 177, 209, 211–12

Ransome-Kuti, Olikoyi, 111, 210

Ransome-Kuti, Olufunmilayo, 92, 95, 105, 111–12, 209–10

  as president of Women's Union, 92, 94–95, 99, 101, 105, 162

regional authority, 33, 100, 102, 118

regional government, 2, 34, 96, 112, 115–16, 118

religion, 18–19, 26, 31, 38, 43, 116, 185, 190, 226, 236

repatriates, xi, 30, 52, 115–16

Rex v. Esther Johnson, 157

Richards, Arthur, 112

Richardson, John, 48

Rock of Abeokuta, 71

Rousseau, Jean-Jacques, 27

  Discours sur l'origine et les fondements de l'inegalite, 27

S

Sacred Heart Hospital, 76

Samuel, J. H., 56

Saro, xii, 12, 17

  alliance with entrepreneurs and the CMS, 55–56

  arrival at Abeokuta, 27, 30, 116, 143

  involvement in Abeokutan politics, xiii, 3–4, 31, 34, 51–53, 55, 61

    nineteenth century, 31, 51–53, 55, 116, 119

    twentieth century, 62, 87, 89, 93, 97, 105, 117, 119

  involvement in regional politics, xiii, 99, 104–5, 118–19

  political interaction with Alake, 51–55, 62

  propagators of modernization, 57

Savage, Emmanuel Akinniyi, 212–13

Savage, Ernestina Modupe, 214

Savage, Gladys Ibidunni, 218

Savage, Josiah Akinbomi, 212

Savage, Michael Akintunde, xv

Savage, Pamela Evelyn, xvi, 149, 218, 220

Savage, Percy, 219

Savage, William Akibo, 149, 217, 220

Savage, William Akilade Kodeleyiri, 218

Schon, J. F., 185

sectional council nominees, 86
sectional Obas, 61, 86–87, 89
Sessarakoo, William Ansah, 27
Sierra Leone, xi, 17, 28, 30, 35, 41,
    115, 184–85, 192, 211, 230,
    238
slaves, manumitted, xii, 17, 28, 34,
    184
slave trade, 5, 27–28, 42, 47, 141,
    143, 184–86, 228, 233, 235
    abolition of, 143, 184
Sodeke (chief of Abeokuta), 13,
    25–26, 30, 44, 143
Sodipo, Adebola, 149
Sodipo, Joseph Deinde, 149
Sogeinbo (balogun), 59, 160
Sokalu, Oba, 44, 99, 145
sole native authority, 3, 13
    Alake as, xii, 86, 116, 119, 197
    See also Ademola II (Alake)
    chair of Egba Central Council as,
        101
Somoye, Segbua, 29, 44, 98, 143
Southeast Asia Contingent Troops
    Reception Committee, 90, 162
Southern Provinces, 86, 88, 100
Soyinka, Oluwole Akinwande, 6, 9,
    149, 210, 220–21
St. John's Anglican Church, 79
suffragettes, 62, 209

T

taxation, 117
    direct, 60, 161
    of women, 92, 94–96, 105, 117,
        162
    tax rate, 113
Taylor, J. C., 185

Tinubu, Madam (Iyalode), 49, 79,
    144, 222–23, 228
Townsend, Henry, 29, 49, 143, 185
township, 20, 54, 61
township councils, 61–62, 86
traditionalists, 53–57, 62, 67
Treaty of Egba Independence, 49

U

unions, 92–93, 96, 209
United Nations, 147, 153, 158, 187,
    195
University of Agriculture, 14, 199
University of Lagos, 15, 199, 206
upper house, xi. See also Western
    House of Chiefs
Usman dan Fodio, 23, 42, 54, 184

W

Warri Province, 88, 91, 162
West African Pilot, 95, 241, 244
Western House of Chiefs, 91, 104, 162
Western Region House of Assembly,
    103
Western Region Local Government
    Law, 104
White, H. F. M., 49
Whitely, Gerald C., 49, 87
Wilberforce, William, 28, 184
Williams, Frederick Rotimi, 224
Women's Union, 92, 96, 104
    conflict with Egba Central Council,
        100–102
    fight against unfair trade practices,
        93–95
    opposition to Alake, 93, 100, 102,
        105, 117, 162, 209

Y

Yar'Adua, Umaru, 203
Yoruba, xi, 3–4, 11–12, 17, 35–39,
        42–43, 45–46, 65, 225–33, 237,
        242
  British impact, 31
  early history, 18, 20–21, 143
    See also Yoruba civil wars
  family life, 18
  language, 3, 49, 144, 185
  spiritual beliefs, 18–19
  traditional political organization,
        19–20, 93
Yoruba civil wars (1820-1828), 22–23,
        54, 65, 115
Yorubaland, 2, 23, 26, 28–29, 32, 46,
        59, 161, 227

Edwards Brothers Malloy
Oxnard, CA USA
July 24, 2013